MEMOIR
ON THE HISTORY OF
THE TOOTH-RELIC OF CEYLON

MEMOIR
ON THE HISTORY OF
THE TOOTH-RELIC OF CEYLON

WITH A PRELIMINARY ESSAY
ON THE

LIFE AND SYSTEM OF GAUTAMA BUDDHA

J. GERSON DA CUNHA

GYAN

Published by

Gyan Publishing House
5, Ansari Road
Daryaganj, New Delhi-110002
Phone: 011-47034999, 9811692060
E-mail: books@gyanbooks.com

Distribution Network
gyanbooks.com
India, USA, Canada, UK, Australia, France

ISBN : 978-81-212-3771-0 (PB)
First Published, London, 1875

2nd Impression 2020

Printed at: Gyan Press, Delhi.

Memoir on the History of the Tooth-Relic of Ceylon
Author: J. Gerson Da Cunha

MEMOIR

ON THE HISTORY OF

THE TOOTH-RELIC OF CEYLON;

WITH A PRELIMINARY ESSAY

ON THE

LIFE AND SYSTEM OF GAUTAMA BUDDHA.

BY J. GERSON DA CUNHA,

Member of the Royal College of Surgeons of England; Licentiate in Midwifery; Licentiate of the Royal College of Physicians of Edinburgh; Fellow of the University of Bombay; Member of the Committee of Management of the Bombay Branch of the Royal Asiatic Society; Member of the British Medical Association, and of the Medical and Physical Society of Bombay; Corresponding Member of the Institute Vasco da Gama, &c. &c.

ILLUSTRATED BY DRAWINGS AND PHOTOGRAPHS.

LONDON: W. THACKER & Co.
CALCUTTA: THACKER, SPINK & Co
MADRAS: HIGGINBOTHAM & Co.
BOMBAY: THACKER, VINING & Co.

1875.

All' Illustrissimo

Signor Avvocato Giuseppe Pilastri,

LAUREATO IN DIRITTO CIVILE E CANONICO NELLA UNIVERSITÀ DI PISA,
CAVALIERE DELL' ORDINE EQUESTRE DEI SS. MAURIZIO E LAZZARO,
CAVALIERE DELL' ORDINE DELLA CORONA D'ITALIA,
DELLA CORONA IMPERIALE DI PRUSSIA,
DECORATO DEL MEDJIDJE DI COSTANTINOPOLI,
DELLA MEDAGLIA COMMEMORATIVA DELLA GUERRA
DELL' INDEPENDENZA ITALIANA,
MEMBRO DELLA SOCIETÀ GEOGRAFICA ITALIANA,
CONSOLE DI SUA MAESTÀ IL RE D'ITALIA IN BOMBAY,
ecc. ecc. ecc.

Carissimo Amico e Signore,

QUANDO incominciai ad occuparmi di alcune ricerche sul Buddhismo, oltre al desiderio d'istruirmi nella sua storia, mi prefissi lo scopo di stabilire un confronto fra i fondatori degli Ordini Monastici nelle Indie ed in Italia.

Gautama Buddha e Francesco d'Assisi hanno tanti punti di contatto e di affinità nelle loro relazioni sociali e morali, che la lettura di tale studio mi sembrò poter riuscire di qualche interesse.

Non avendo altro ad offrirle se non che questo povero libro, spoglio affatto di pregi, io lo dedico a Lei qual pegno di verace amicizia, augurandomi ch'Ella vorrà fargli buon viso avuto riguardo all' animo dell' amico, che nell' offerta chiede indulgenza più assai che lode.

Descrivo in questo mio libro un periodo glorioso nella storia delle Indie, e dovendo in esso dar qualche cenno di Antichità, Poesia, Scultura e Pittura, più facilmente m' indussi a dedicarlo a Lei figlio della Terra che vide nascere Virgilio, Dante, Michelangelo, Raffaello, Guicciardini, Vico, Romagnosi e gli altri molti che illustrarono con le loro opere il mondo.

Parlo dell' antica India che nella storia ha pagine incancellabili; della moderna non dico, di questa "Ai posteri l'ardua sentenza."

Mi conservi l' affetto che sempre mi ha dimostrato e mi creda di cuore

affmo. amico,

J. GERSON DA CUNHA.

Bombay, 29 *Maggio* 1875.

TABLE OF CONTENTS.

VII.—ON THE RELICS OF BUDDHA.

How the innumerable relics of Buddha are preserved—The relics of the disciples of Buddha—The tooth of Buddha.

VIII.—THE AUTHORITIES ON THE HISTORY OF THE TOOTH-RELIC OF CEYLON.

The neglect of the study of the history of the *dalada* or tooth-relic of Ceylon—The earliest and authentic records of the tooth-relic—The Dhâtuvañśa—Difficulties in assigning a fixed date to this Buddhist chronicle—The translations of the Dhâtuvañśa.

IX.—THE HISTORY OF THE TOOTH IN INDIA.

How the tooth was picked up from the funeral pyre of Buddha—The indignities it was subjected to by the Emperor Pâṇḍu—The miracles wrought by the tooth—Its removal to Ceylon.

X.—THE ARRIVAL OF THE TOOTH IN CEYLON.

How the Dhâtadhâtu festival was celebrated—The removal of the tooth to Madura—Its restoration.

XI.—ITS CAPTURE BY THE PORTUGUESE.

How D. Constantino da Bragança got possession of the tooth in the temple of Jaffnapatam—The narrative of Diogo do Couto—The embassy the king of Pegu sent to Goa for its purchase—The answer they got from the Viceroy.

XII.—ITS DESTRUCTION BY THE ARCHBISHOP.

How Archbishop Don Gaspar prevailed upon D. Constantino to refuse the handsome offer of the king of Pegu—How the tooth was pounded, burnt, and scattered in the waters of a running stream—Then a scutcheon made to commemorate the event.

XIII.—CONTEMPORARY OPINION ON THE EVENT.

The opinion of Cottineau—That of Padre Francisco de Souza.

PREFACE.

The ideas and facts comprised in this volume are principally drawn from materials for a memoir which I had recently the honour of communicating to the Bombay Branch of the Royal Asiatic Society.

Its reproduction in a more accessible form here from the Journal of that learned Society is, however, fraught with one disadvantage—that the fortunes of Gautama Buddha's tooth are in general too remote from the sympathies of those not professing his creed to find favour with them, especially on account of the spirit of the marvellous pervading almost every page of the Buddhist religious records, already too wearisome from their chronically labouring under what Macaulay would call the "Lues Boswelliana," or disease of admiration, for every object pandering to the worship of Śâkya Muni.

In connection, however, with an account of the life and system of the eminent Hindu sage, involving as they do problems of deep concern to the philosopher and the religionist, and throwing light on an obscure period—the morning-twilight of Indian authentic history—it greatly enhances the value of that 'paper,' and deserves the attentive study of every one taking an interest in the moral and religious history of our species.

But even though that remarkable period during which Gautama Buddha flourished had nothing extraordinary to interest us, the attractive beauty of his life, and the great influence exercised till the present day over an immense section of mankind by his system—an offshoot though it be of the Indian mind, not in the fresh days of its prime and vigour, but at a memorable epoch when the Âryan feudalism, so to speak, tracing back its origin to an economical law lying at the very root of Indian society, was slowly yielding to the incessant revolutionary movement of the aboriginal Turanian serfs, and the Vedas with their exclusive doctrines were no longer capable of controlling the multitudes that had apparently become too unwieldy to be guided by it—would in themselves be sufficient to do so. In other climes and countries exempted from the domain of arbitrary and anomalous ordinances governing the Indian people, an achievement of this sort would perhaps have eventually led to a better political organization, and the day of its inauguration marked as a gala day in the annals of nations. In India, however, in a country without a parallel in the course its social and religious institutions have run, the effect of the impetus seems to have been rebounding; it found the people too firmly incased to burst forth, in spite of the salutary pressure applied to it, with a new, young life. One reaction was followed by another, until at last their resultant was an evident retrogression.

To render, however, such a subject interesting, it necessitates, besides an able exposition requiring the qualifications of an Eugène Burnouf or of the veteran Hodgson, the mastering of volumes in half a dozen Eastern languages, written in so many different characters,—a task that it is the privilege of few to perform to one's satisfaction.

As my work has grown from a simple memoir, so has grown my interest in it, and, although the present work is concluded, I do not feel inclined to lay aside the study. The subject, however, is really so extensive, that, in spite of the care and labour bestowed by me in the few hours I could snatch from a laborious medical practice during its preparation, errors, I am afraid, have crept in, especially regarding those points in Buddhism which are still controversial.

In conclusion I would merely further remark, although it may appear superfluous to do so, that within the narrow sphere of a memoir and an essay I could not possibly do more than give a faint outline of a vast field of research, in which only the prominent events in the life of Buddha are sketched, and his system dealt with more from a synthetic than from an analytical point of view, avoiding as much as possible whatever might savour of dogmatism concerning the views I have expressed; while in narrating the events connected with the history of the relic, I have given impartially the data that impugn its genuineness, without meaning any offence to those who believe in it. How far I have succeeded in these particulars is left to the decision of others. Should it, however, induce subsequent researches in this comparatively neglected field of study, it will amply repay me for the hours I have sedulously spent in writing the following pages.

A PRELIMINARY ESSAY

ON THE

LIFE AND SYSTEM OF GAUTAMA BUDDHA.

It may not perhaps be generally known that, like the two Kâlidâsas, there are two historical personages who alike claim the honour of being called Gautama Buddha, to say nothing of a great number of others bearing their name but devoid of their fame. They are what the philologist calls homonyms, but not homogenes. One is a great writer on dialectics, his system being the most excellent that Indian logicians have ever produced;* the other is the celebrated propounder of the religious system known as Buddhism, who, though he delivered many discourses and preached a good deal, never wrote, like the other great reformers of old, a word that could be transmitted to posterity. It is the latter personage who is the subject of the following observations.

We learn from the *Lalita-Vistâra*,† a legendary biography of Buddha in Sanskṛit, that Buddha was born with certain peculiarities of body and mind which indicated, according to the contemporary soothsayers, that he was destined to attain preëminence in the realms of politics or religion. As is generally the case with extraordinary personages of antiquity, his birth was preceded by extraordinary phenomena, and followed by other not less remarkable circumstances, that foreshadowed his future greatness. While still in the womb, his mother, the handsome and accomplished princess Mâyâ-Devî, 'divine delusion,' had

---

* *Dictionnaire des Sciences Philosophiques par une Soc. de Prof. de Philosophie*, Paris, 1845, Art. 'Gotama.'

† Ph. Ed. Foucaux's *Texte Tibétain* of *Tch'er Ryga Rol Pa* (*Lalita-Vistâra*), vol. ii., Paris, 1847-48; *Partie du Chapitre* VII., Paris, 1841; R. Lenz's *Analyse du Lalita-Vistâra-pourana*, St. Petersbourg, 1836; and Râjendralâl Mittra's *Lalita-Vistâra*, Calcutta, 1853. The *Lalita-Vistâra*, which literally means "the development of plays," is supposed to have been written by one of the principal disciples of Buddha soon after his death, and in accordance with accounts as given by himself; hence it is considered to be the most reliable source regarding the life of the great reformer. It was translated into Chinese in the year 76 A.D.

a dream of the White Elephant descending on her from the *Tushita*,* or the joyful heavens; and as the period of confinement drew near she asked permission of her husband Śuddhodana, the allegorical signification of whose name is 'he whose food is pure,' and who is described as a just and pious man, to visit her father Su-prabuddah, during which she gave birth to the great Gautama in a standing posture while holding the branches of a tree in the *Lumbîni* garden. The moment he is born he is taken charge of by the great Brahmâ in the 'golden net,' or curtain of stars, who, presenting him to his mother, exclaims, "Happy art thou, O queen, whose son hath merit beyond all comparison."† From the hands of the great Brahmâ he is received by the four guardians of the world, from them by the archangel Indra, and from the latter by a host of Brâhmaṇs. Then follow predictions. The child is in a short time receiving the homage of all the wise men of the country, walks by his own power, looks in various directions, and with an admirable display of precocity cries out, "I am the most exalted in the world. Hereafter there is to me no other birth."‡

---

* *Tushita* or *Tusita*, the fourth heaven out of the six, where Bodhisatvas, or beings destined to become Buddhas, dwell. It is believed that the *Patra* or Alms-pot, the Holy Grail of Buddhism, was taken up into that place, which ascension was held to be indicative of the disappearance of the Law from the earth's surface, to be restored by the future Buddha Maitreya. The restoration was looked forward to by the Buddhist with as much anxiety as the coming of the Messiah by the Jew of old, and perhaps by the modern too. The *patra* is now shown in the Maligâva Vihâra at Kandy.

† A parody of the Hail Mary? The parallel can be carried a little further. We are told by travellers that both in Japan and in China all around the temples there are shrines supporting the diminutive figures in bronze of Mâyâ-Devî, the virgin mother of Buddha, which theologians hold to be a modern innovation, derived from the early Christian Church, analagous to that of the Madonna, whose statuettes with an infant in her arms are sold in these countries as those of the mother of Buddha. In the fabulous legend of *Lao-tse*, composed in 350 A.D., Gautama is said to have issued miraculously from the left side of his mother, who carried him for seventy-two years in her womb, and died seven days after his birth—a theory of incarnation that was subsequently shared by the Valentinians. St. Jerome tells us that a story had reached him, and was repeated by Ratvamnus, respecting the birth of Gautama from the side of a virgin. (Lassen, *Ind. Alt.*, vol. iii., p. 370.) Others state that he was first a Bodhisatva, and to rise to the dignity of a Buddha it was necessary for him to become incarnate as the son of Mâyâ. (St. Julien, *Lao-tse*, p. xxiii.)

‡ Only the most succinct account of the Buddhist legendary lore can be given here; details are found in the Rev. Spence Hardy's *Life of Buddha*, Lond. 1866; Henry Alabaster's *Wheel of the Law*, Lond. 1871; *Asiatic Researches*, vol. ii., pp. 333 *et seq.*; Madame Mary Summer's *Histoire du Bouddha-Sakya-Mouni*, Paris, 1873; Koeppen's *Die Religion des Buddha und ihre Entstehung*, Berlin, 1857; St. Hilaire's *Du Bouddhisme*, &c., Paris, 1855; Bigandet's *Life or Legend of Gaudama*, Rangoon, 1866. Those who wish to look on the subject from a poetical standpoint may read an epic entitled *The Story of Gautama Buddha and his Creed*, by R. Phillips, Lond. 1871.

Gautama Buddha was born in 624 B.C.,* at Kapila or Kapila-

* The Indian Buddhists and the people of Ava, Siam, and Ceylon, fix the above date as that of his birth; but the Kashmirians place it about 1332 B.C., the Japanese and Mongols about 1000 B.C.; while the Tibetans vary it between 2959 and 400 B.C. In the *Ain-i-Akbari* we are informed that Buddha was born 2962 years before the period at which the author wrote, which was the 40th year of the reign of Akbar, *i.e.* 1596 of our era; consequently Buddha must have been born 1366 B.C., but on no grounds—mythological, traditional, or historical—can the honour of such a high antiquity be admitted. Again, the Chinese accounts tell us that Gautama was born on the 8th day of the 4th month and 24th year of the reign of Tchao-Wang of the Tcheou dynasty, *i. e.* 1029 B.C. (Des Guignes, Abel Rémusat, and Klaproth, *Mélanges Asiatiques*, tome i., pp. 113-117, and *Nouveau Journal Asiatique*, tome xii.). These discrepancies may probably be accounted for by these different peoples confounding the original legislator with the Buddhas who have preceded or succeeded him at divers long intervals. But I have heard nothing so astounding, betraying at the same time an absolute want of critical power, or rather of diplomatic criticism, so essential to the fair interpretation of ancient texts, as the attempt lately made in a learned society to prove that the founder of Buddhism was born only 31 years before that revivalist of Brahmanism the well-known Sankarâchârya. (See the *Journal of the Institute Vasco da Gama*, vol. iii., p. 176.) The arguments put forth are mostly founded upon a text derived from *Kalpalatikâ*, a Sanskṛit work said to have been written, according to some, by Mâdhava Vidyâranya, who flourished in the 13th century of the Śâlivâhana era, while the work itself bears the date 1012 of the same era, and is according to others written by another Mâdhava. Now the text is this:—नवेंदतर्कप्रमितेशालिवाहनजन्मत: जातोमंडणमिश्राख्योबुन्धो नास्तिक्यकारक: *i.e.* "in the year 619 of the Śâlivâhana era the atheist Buddha, named Mandana Miśra, was born." According to the same authority, Śankarâchârya was born 650 S., which corresponds to 729 A.D., 729 — 31 = 698; hence Buddha was born only six hundred and ninety-eight years after Christ, a date which is in flagrant contradiction with all that is known to us of Aśoka edicts and other Buddhist inscriptions. The mistake evidently arises from assuming the word Buddha, which is merely an epithet, and may perhaps be likened to our modern 'doctor' or 'professor,' to be a proper noun. The text besides tells us that the Buddha atheist he writes about is Mandana Miśra, a Hindu philosopher also known under the names of Sureśvarâchârya and Viśva-Rûpâchârya, the author of a *Vârttika*, or an explanatory gloss to a philosophical Sûtra, who is so entirely distinct from Gautama Buddha as to preclude all possibility of doubt. Some French writers consider the above date as erroneous, and founded on the perplexing Sinhalese chronology. M. Rodier says: "C'est en 1834, avant notre ère, que naquit Siddarata, qui a reçu plus tard le surnom de Bouddha." (*Antiquité de Races Humaines*, p. 354.) "Quelque embrouillée que soit la chronologie ceylanaise, elle suffirait à elle seule pour faire voir l'absurdité du calcul rétrospectif qui a donné ce chiffre .... les Ceylanais ont confondu, en un seul personnage, deux Bouddhas bien distincts." (*Ibid.* pp. 361, 362.) I have adopted the generally received chronology, as given in the text. I may also advert *en passant* to the fact of some persons identifying Buddha with the prophet Daniel, and ascribing the appearance of his system in India to the captivity and dispersion of the Jews, to say nothing of his being the St. Josaphat of the Greek and Roman Churches, who was a prince, a hermit, and a saint at the same time. For more particulars on this subject the reader may consult Wilson's paper in the *Journal of the Royal Asiatic Society*, 1856, vol. xvi., p. 233; Colonel Yule's edition of *Marco Polo's Travels*, vol. ii., p. 263; and Prof. Max Müller's article on *The Migration of Fables* in the *Contemporary Review*, July 1870.

vastû,* at the foot of the mountains of Nepâl, the present site of the town of Nagara, near the river Ghoghra, about a hundred miles north of the holy city of Benares, the Athens of Hindustân.† He belonged to the family of the Śâkyas,‡ or 'self-potential,' by which patronymic he is often named, with the suffix of Muni (a devotee or an ascetic), or with that of Siñha, 'a lion,' peculiar to the military class: hence Śâkyamuni means an anchorite of the family of the Śâkyas. He is also named Sacya Siñha, or Scythian Lion. The fancied etymology of the latter name, combined with the sculptured appearances of Gautama, has given rise among some writers to speculations about the originator of Buddhism not being a native of Hindustân, but of Scythia or Abyssinia. Sir W. Jones was the first to suggest that the curled and woolly appearance of the hair on the head of the statues of Buddha, many of which are sculptured in the black granite or basalt of Western India, indicated African descent. (*As. Res*, vol. i., p. 427.) Langlès, in his *Monumens de l'Hindoustan*, Paris, 1821, vol. i., pp. 186 and 206, maintains the same opinion. Such doubts may have been allowable perhaps when materials for forming a correct judgment were still wanting, but now that his origin has been established beyond all controversy by native authorities, as interpreted by Hodgson, we have no longer left us any ground for such a disputation. (*As. Res.* vol. vii., p. 314.) Among the thirty-two *lakshaṇas* or characteristics, and eighty *vianjanas* or peculiar signs of beauty or personal appearance of Gautama Buddha, we meet with *svarṇa-varṇaḥ* or golden complexion, and *tunga-nâsikaḥ* or aquiline nose, which are certainly not negro features. (Rémusat, *Mélanges Asiatiques*, vol. vi., p. 100.) Curly locks are considered, besides, by natives a point of beauty, odd though the fact may appear to a sect that insists on tonsure.

---

* Kapila, of a part of which the father of Buddha was king, and tributary to that of Kośala, was built by the deported sons of Ikshvâku by the permission of the sage Kapila, whence the name. Another version is to the effect that Kapilavastu means *yellow dwelling*, and yellow appears to have been the distinctive colour of the principality; and hence it may have been adopted as the badge of the Buddhists, who are sometimes spoken of as of the yellow religion. Chy-Fa-Hian, the well-known Chinese Buddhist pilgrim of the fourth century, has left us in his narrative a description of the place as it was then.

† See for particulars General Cunningham's *Ancient Geography of India*, Lond. 1871, pp. 414 *et seq.*

‡ The Śâkyas were descendants of Ikskvâku, and formed one of the branches of the Solar dynasty, who reigned in the Śâkya country. They are also said to be the descendants of *Arkabandhu*, which in the Glossary of Amarasiñha is given as a synonym of Buddha.

During his youth he appears to have led a life of secular pursuits and pleasure, being distinguished for skill in all sorts of manly sports, especially in the use of the bow, one particular feat having been handed down to us and commemorated on one of the Elliot Marbles. Notwithstanding all the distractions of the court, he was also much addicted to a contemplative life. Some of his expressions in youthful days, at a time when a boy usually misbehaves himself, gets into scrapes, and is yet learning, reveal Gautama as very punctilious, and of an exceedingly cheerless disposition. "Nothing is stable on earth," he used to say, "nothing is real. Life is like the spark produced by the friction of wood."* His high destiny and the objects that would move him to adopt the ascetic life having been foretold, he had for years been confined in three palaces built specially for him, within the limits of which the young prince was to pass the three seasons of the year, guards being posted to bar the approach of the dreaded objects. All these precautions, however, were of no avail against inevitable destiny and the power of the Devas.

On going out of the gate on three or more occasions he saw certain objects which led him to think on death and the vanity of the world. One of these was a decrepit old man with broken teeth, grey locks, form bending towards the ground, and his trembling steps supported by a staff. A Deva had taken this form. The young prince inquired of his charioteer whether the man was born so, and the charioteer replied that he was once young like himself. After several other questions he asked at last whether he also would become old and feeble, and was told that it was a state at which all beings must arrive. Four months later the princesaw a leper, and again, after the same lapse of time, a dead body in a state of decomposition. Lastly he saw a religious recluse radiant with peace and tranquillity, which made a lasting impression on his mind.

Before the attainment of Buddha-hood or omniscience Gautama was called Savartha-Siddha, afterwards abbreviated into Siddhârtha, a Sanskṛit word meaning 'one whose objects have been effected,' which appellation he appears to have used in his youth. In some Pâli works he is also called Siddhatta, 'the establisher.' His title

* Conf. our Saviour's words, *Quid enim prodest homini si mundum universum lucretur, animæ vero ejus detrimentum patiatur*, so happily used by Loyola in the initiation of St. Francis Xavier.

of Buddha,* 'the enlightened,' 'the sanctified,' was given to him when he attained to wisdom, the word being of Sanskṛit origin, बुध (*budha*), derived from बुध् (*budh*), 'to know, fathom, penetrate;' and Gautama the name of the clan or race to which his family belonged. At the age of sixteen he married his cousin, the beautiful Yasodhara, elsewhere named Gopa, daughter of Śuddhodana's sister Amita and of Daṇḍapâni the king of Koli; but it was not till his twenty-ninth year that she bore him a son, when, casting one glance at them, to whom he was tenderly attached, he left the palace suddenly at night accompanied by his faithful attendant Chandaka, whom he afterwards dismissed, to betake himself to the forests of Magadha, one of the most polished provinces of Central India, and, far away from all that could bind by affection or attract by smile, to become a voluntary exile.

This was the turning-point of his career. He was now free to give ample scope to those various metaphysical views which he had so long secretly cherished in his mind. When quite a boy he was much inclined to meditation, and, although nurtured in the midst of luxury, was growing weary of the pomp and pleasures of his father's court, and the symptoms of threefold decline—religious, moral, and political—which India presented at that period could not have escaped his ob-

---

* The names of Buddha are legion. He is sometimes called Sugata, 'the well-gone,' as it literally means; to avoid tautology they again address him as Tathagata, 'the thus-gone;' 'the five-eyed,' *i. e.* the eyes of flesh, divine eyes, eyes of wisdom, the special eye of a Buddha, and the omniscient eye. Then he is called Bhagava, in the sense in which we use the expression 'our Lord' or 'our Saviour.' He is the Κατέξοχην and Σαρμάναι of the Greeks, Bud or Wud of the Arabs, Mercurius of the Romans,—although this latter name is said to be more applicable to Budha the son of Soma and regent of the planet Mercury, 'one who knows,' than to Buddha, 'the deified mortal,' two distinct persons (see Taylor, *Hindu Mythology*, 26, and Wilson, *Vishṇu Purâṇa*, pp. 393-394). He is also the *Mayæ filius* of Horace; he is said to correspond with the Woden of the Scandinavians, Toth of the Egyptians, Fo of the Chinese, Pont of the Siamese, Kokaka of the Japanese, Chakabout of the Tonquinese, Chomdondas of the Tibetans, and Burkhan (Budha?) of the Mongols, among whom the third day of the week, *Dies Mercurii*, or Wednesday, is dedicated to him. It is also said that Jagannâtha, or 'lord of the universe,' is an appellation that Gautama himself assumed, for on the day he became Buddha, and also when he was about to expire, he exclaimed, "O universe, I am thy lord." This name has doubtless some connection with the Jagganâtha pilgrimage, for within the sacred precincts of this deity all classes are privileged to meet, which savours of a Buddhistic origin.

By Brâhmaṇs he is considered the ninth *avatâr* of Vishṇu, and the claim seems to have been conceded, for Jayadeva in the *Gîta Govinda* has admitted it, though when Buddhism, gathering strength, began to persecute the old Vaishṇavas, the claim was denied, and Balabhadra, the nominal brother of Kṛishṇa, chosen instead.

serving eyes. "Solitude," says a great man that recently departed from amongst us, "is essential to any depth of meditation or of character, and which in the presence of natural beauty and grandeur is the cradle of thought and aspiration."* The wilderness was then the fittest retreat for Buddha to commune with himself, and it would not be difficult for one to hazard an opinion about what thoughts must then have revolved in his mind on the 'fair pretexts and gorgeous devices' invented for the existence of an overruling and absolute sacerdotalism in which the ethnic principle of tribe and clan was the predominating element, and which the subject-races felt as the most grievous oppression, without any one to raise a cry for the restoration of liberty and emancipation!

If we were to believe the epics of India, and their still extremely problematical chronology, we might count upon as facts that the Solar race entered India about 1000 years before the Lunar race, and the latter about the 13th century B.C. From this time until the 4th century B.C. no horde of any race, so far as we are aware, appears to have crossed the Indus. By this time, too, the story of a people migrating from far beyond the snow-clad mountains, where the gods are thought to hold their councils, into the vast plains of Hindustân, was probably long forgotten, and the blood of the Âryans got mixed with that of the aborigines. And moreover, as the swarms of the Âryan race advanced in a southerly direction, the monotheism of the Vedas became infected by the legends and superstitions of the Drâviḍian people; the purer doctrine of the priesthood and ecclesiastical polity of the days of the *Ṛig-Veda* and *Mânava-Dharma-Sâstra* was superseded by the avarice, licentiousness, and cruelty of the Brâhmaṇs; the military class, mostly consisting of criminals; and parricides ruling the turbulent kingdoms of Central India; the hierarchy of caste holding the conquered Ṭâmil races in complete serfdom, and instruction being looked upon more as the monopoly of the privileged classes than as the heritage of mankind.

Though vanquished in arms, the defeated party, now awakened to the sense of their dignity, were no longer prepared to see with indifference their inferiority paraded as an article of religious faith, and it was too clear that if an advocate of the equality of men of every race *coram lege* were to appear and proclaim it without the least fear of the Brâhmaṇs—who though unblameable for maintaining the superiority

* J. Stuart Mill, *Political Economy*, iii.

of talent and energy which has always been their appanage, could not deny to the aboriginal races the right to rise to any position of which they were capable—he might surely calculate without any misgiving on their espousing the cause, and rallying round him.

This state of things could not really last long; the times were ripe for the advent of a reformer, and only a genius like that of Śakyamuni, burning with love for his countrymen and for the human race in general—a young man of gentle, ardent, and philanthropic nature, with presentiments and ever-darkening pictures of the wickedness of the world before him, mourning over the prostration of mankind,—could awake to the idea of standing forth in the capacity of a liberator; and endowed as he was with a handsome figure, suavity of manners, and touching eloquence of address, with which he imparted to his followers the moral grandeur of his opinions and his designs, and inflamed them with it, he seemed really to be predestined to play the grand *rôle* he did. But all his efforts to enter on this noble mission were unavailing until the young ascetic, by the influence of his own merit, overcoming all trials and temptations; enduring those preliminary contests, spiritual and physical, under which ordinary mortals succumb; running counter to the wishes of his father and of his young wife, and exchanging the honours and magnificence of the court for the want, privations, and hardships of a hermit's cave, had sat for seven years under a *Bo*-tree* in the forest of Uruwela by the river Nairanjana, and, entirely abstracted in meditations, had raised himself at last to the true condition of a Buddha. This took place in the year 588 B.C., and in the thirty-sixth year of his age.

In the privations of the forest the Hindu sage learnt the effect of temperance upon the mind, fitting it for quiet contemplation; and from concentrating all his mental faculties on one single object as his own being, he was led by this process to look upon man as a mere *rupa*,

* The *Bo*-tree is the Sacred Fig-tree or *pimpal*, the *Ficus religiosa* of botanists. Under that tree, supposed to be in the centre of what is called Bodhimaṇḍala, a circle of hypothetical extent in the Indian peninsula, Buddha sat during meditations that made him omniscient. It is the sacred tree of the Buddhists, and found in the grounds of almost every temple. Moreover, according to the popular mythology, each Buddha had his own favourite tree; thus the Bo or Bodhi tree of the first Buddha of the present age was *Sirisa* (*Acacia Sirisa*); that of the second was *Udumbara* (*Ficus glomerata*); that of the third was *Nyagrodha* (*Ficus indica*). Burnouf writes: "Cela prouve que le nom de Bodhi est un terme générique désignant l'arbre sous lequel un Buddha doit obtenir la consécration de sa mission sublime, et non pas le nom propre et populaire de cette espèce de figuier."—*Introd. à l'Hist. du Buddhisme Indien*, Paris, 1844, p. 388.

an organized body endowed with certain attributes, and perhaps, like Dr. Holbach, upon nature as a machine, morality as self-interest, and deity as a fiction; the reason of man his safest guide, and the law of nature perfect justice in the whole creation. However, he had in ideas and sentiments great elevation and magnanimity, hatred of all that is low and mean, of every systematic sham and organized hypocrisy, which then, more than now, were the order of the day. Gautama was in this respect but a feeble reflection of the great Galilæan, who, attracting towards him, on the margins of the Lake of Gennesareth, in Palestine, large crowds of the people, instilling into them his own enthusiasm, being identified with their joys and sorrows, and constituting himself their champion and friend, converted them into his most devoted followers. It was in this solitude, then, that Gautama Buddha nourished his mighty heart with thoughts that held happiness to be the reward of a course of undeviating rectitude, and undisturbed serenity of a steady observance of the path of duty.

The portentous agitation in the moral world so happily inaugurated by Gautama Buddha was not confined to India alone. It was a time pregnant with events of universal moment, when Ezekiel was receiving his commission as a prophet, and members of the Hebrew commonwealth honoured with the keeping of Holy Writ were fast dropping into the grasp of the Babylonic despots, their sanctuary profaned, their liturgy suspended, and the city of Jerusalem itself reduced by Nebuchadnezzar to a heap of ruins. In Greece, where Solon was busy in legislating for Athens, a young and ardent people, under the salutary influence of Anacreon, Epimenides, Pisistratus and others, was rising to eminence in arts and sciences, and founding that Hellenic speculation which was about to commence its struggles for the disenthralment of the human mind; while Rome under Servius Tullius was borrowing from Etruria her first elements of civilization, which were destined at a later period to change the demi-savage aspect of the erratic sons of Gaul and Germania into a new civilizing power; and swarms of Orphic brotherhoods, and the fresh creations of Thrace, Egypt, and Phrygia were seeking an objective revelation of God's will. In China a successful movement had just been organized by Confucius in the rehabilitating of the ancient state religion; and Persia under Cyrus was the theatre of changes still more decisive, expressing her consciousness of antagonism among the elements of our moral being by the Zoroastrian theory of the two rival principles of Hormazd and Ahriman.

But to return to our narrative. Siddhârtha, issuing forth from the solitude of Uruwela as the great Buddha, the successor of Kakusandha, Kanagamana, and Kaśyapa, the fourth of the present age of Buddha-Kalpa,* and a worthy representative of the twenty-four others of the past cycle, assuming the name of Gautama Buddha, commenced to teach and preach those tenets which resulted in the foundation of the mendicant order of Buddhists,† and in that system of religious belief—if belief is not a misnomer for a religion of cold and blank negations—which has, in spite of all its dreariness, won the allegiance of the teeming millions of the East, and has, doubtless, exerted, and is still exerting, so beneficent and humanizing an influence on nearly a third of the human family, inhabiting diverse climes and countries; for Buddha's name is revered as much in the palm-groves of Ceylon, the swarming hives of the Chinese towns, and the elegant gardens of Japan, as in the mountain-passes of Nepâl, the shady valleys of Cashmere, the wild frontiers of the great deserts of Tibet and Mongolia, and the scorching shores of the trans-Gangetic provinces of India.

Having practised rigorous asceticism for seven years and preached for forty-five at Benares, Râjagriha, the capital of Magadha, and other places, during which period the record of his life is one long catalogue of good—his time occupied in the relief of the wretched, the care of his disciples, and in the continual practice of those virtues which his precepts inculcated—the great Indian reformer, feeling that his time for leaving the earth and attaining *nirvâṇa* was approaching, gave a charge to his assembled disciples:—"Priests," said he, "if

* There is no doubt that the Kalpas have been borrowed in their entirety by the Buddhists from the Brâhmans; and the idea of Buddha as a teacher of mankind is founded upon a supposed perpetual and invariable rotation of series of ages. This round of ages making a great Kalpa is said to have been completed already eleven times, and Buddha has often been incarnate to promote "the disentanglement of human spirits from the vortex of illusion:" E. Salisbury, *Jour. Amer. Or. Soc.* vol. i., p. 86. The Kalpas are besides distinguished by gradual decrease of man's life and stature in each of its yugas. In the first yuga the average duration of man's life was 80,000, in the second 10,000, in the third 1,000; in the present, we are told, it will go on diminishing from 100 to 7, while the stature will eventually dwindle down to the height of a thumb! It is consoling to know, however, that the time is still, to us, far off; perhaps it was not so to the Lilliputians of Gulliver.

† "L'Inde est, plus que les autres régions, propice à une semblable confrérie, à cause de son excellent climat, de la richesse de sa nature, et des faibles besoins qu'éprouve la vie de l'homme. Dans tous les siècles elle s'est distinguée par sa générosité, en entretenant à ses frais une foule innombrable des sectaires différents, des parasites, comme encore aujourd'hui."—Vassilief's *Bouddisme*, traduit du Russe par M. Lacomme, Paris, 1865, p. 15.

you have any doubts regarding the doctrines I have taught you for five and forty years, you have permission to declare them now, otherwise you may regret that you had not the opportunity of stating them whilst I was yet in existence; or, if you hesitate to make known your doubts to me, make them known to one another." As the priests did not entertain any doubts, they held their peace, and Gautama proceeded:—"Are there no doubts that you wish to have removed? Then I depart to *nirvāṇa*. I leave with you my ordinances. The elements of the omniscient will pass away, but the truth, the word, and the priesthood will remain." Thus having spoken, the great reformer, at the advanced age of eighty-one, while about to enter the town of Kuśinagara, modern Kasia, on the margin of the Atchiravati, one of the branches of the Ganges, turned round to his faithful companion Ânandà, and before crossing the river glanced at the place and exclaimed: "It is for the last time that I contemplate from a distance the city of Râjagriha and the throne of diamonds;" he then retired to Kuśinagara, and entered a grove of *sál*-trees (*Shorea robusta*) there. During the night he received a gift of food from an artizan named Chanda and was seized with illness. At early dawn next day, as he turned on to his right side with his head to the north, the *sál*-trees bending down to form a canopy over his body, he ceased to breathe.* This event occurred in the full-moon of Vaiśâkh or May of the year 543 B.C.,—about two centuries before the arrival of Alexander's expedition in India. His obsequies were attended by a large concourse of the inhabitants of the city, and his mortal remains burnt upon a magnificent funeral pile with all due solemnity, and the ashes and bones that survived the cremation treasured by his disciples and by kings.

Soon after Buddha's death the necessity for collecting his various doctrines, which till then had been only orally promulgated, was felt; and, as sects and dissensions soon arose among his followers, it was resolved to fix for the future the Buddhistic canon containing the *ipsissima verba* of Gautama.†

* William Knighton notes:—"Alas for the dignity of this mightiest and most widely-spread of religions! his death was caused, according to tradition, by the eating of pork!"—*Forest Life in Ceylon*, Lond. 1854, vol. ii., p. 21. But this appears to be a Brahmanical sarcasm; for if true, it looks rather as the *dénouement* of a Sybarite's career, a more fitting termination of a gay Lothario's life than that of a meditative recluse like Gautama Buddha.

† Otto Kistner's *Buddha and his Doctrines*, Lond. 1869, p. 1.

During his lifetime no such code was needed,—the presence of the great master was enough, and thoughts of his removal by death from the scene of his labours hardly appear to have entered into the calculations of his followers. It was only when Buddha was elevated to the beatific stage of *nirváṇa* that his disciples attempted to place on record the words and deeds of their departed teacher. Everything that redounded to the glory of Gautama Buddha was eagerly welcomed, while all that detracted from the ideal they had formed of him was unhesitatingly rejected.* The compilation of his system was carried on not only in secrecy—no critic, stranger, or even priest except a select few being allowed in the councils of the wise; for it is plainly written in the *Mahâvaṅsa*, p. 12, *Naunchitatha vatthabbam iti*, "it cannot be allowed to other priests to be present"—but with expedition, lest the spirit of nonconformity, which had so early begun to make its appearance, should threaten the stability of the Buddhist edifice.

Like the Christian Fathers, the Buddhist doctors assembled in general councils or convocations, which were severally held at Râjagriha, in Berâr, Vesali (modern Allahâbâd), and Pâṭaliputra (modern Pâṭṇâ), the Nicæa of Buddhism.† The first, attended by five hundred monks, was held within two months after Buddha's death, in the reign of Adjatasattru, the son of Bimbisara, who was a great supporter of Buddhism, and was murdered by his son seven years previous to Buddha's death, to gain the throne, and was presided over by the renowned Kâśyapa, the Buddhist primate; the second in 443 B.C., when Kâlâśoka was the king of Maghada (Behâr); and the third in 309 B.C., or about 235 years after Śâkyamuni's death, in the reign of that great protector of Buddhism, King Aśoka the Just, under the presidency of Maggalipata, who was then seventy years old. The reign of the latter monarch bears to the Buddhistic religion a relation similar to that which the reign of Constantine does to the Christian Church, they both elevating their faith into the state religion, the only difference being that while the universal council held at Nicæa in 325 A.D. was the first, that at Pâṭaliputra was the third. The object of holding the council was the device to establish perfect unity in the practice of discipline

* Max Müller's *Lectures on the Science of Religion*, Lond. 1874, pp. 29-32.

† The latest synod of the Buddhist clergy we have notice of was convened in the year 1867 at the town of Palmadulla, in Ceylon, for fixing the text of the *Sûtras* and *Piṭakas*.—*The Academy*, August 15, 1871, p. 407.

among the religious, and to come to an agreement on the subject of the genuineness of the scriptures. The edicts of King Payadasi (Aśoka) inscribed on the *lâṭs* or pillars, and blocks of granite, which commemorate his reign, exhibit him at first as tolerant and friendly towards both the Brâhmaṇs and Buddhist Samanas or Śramanas* (monks), but at last as a complete Buddhist. His conversion marks an era in Buddhist propagandism. The new religion was as yet confined to comparatively few adherents and a small extent of territory; but, with the proverbial zeal, though without the intolerance, of a neophyte, he employed all his tact and resources in furthering vast missionary enterprises, which spread Buddhism far beyond the frontiers of India.

The *Tripiṭaka*, the Threefold Treasure or Three Baskets, which became the rule of faith for the millions who came thus thereafter to believe in it, was divided into three sections; the first being called *Sûtra* or *Sutta-Piṭaka*, containing discourses of Buddha, devoted to the inculcation and illustration of moral truth, principally collected by Ânanda; the second, *Vinaya-Piṭaka*, containing the regulations of the priesthood or the discipline and daily life of the priests, by Upali; and the third, *Abhidharma-Piṭaka*, the so-called by-laws addressed to the beings of the immaterial world, by Mahâkaśyapa. The latter two divisions, containing works on dogmatic philosophy and metaphysics, the essence of Buddhaic faith, are often styled *Dharmas*. By the Chinese Buddhists the above three divisions are called, in short, Sacred Books, Precepts, and Discourses.† These *Piṭakas* are accompanied by what is called *Attahakattas* or commentaries, translated with additions into Pâli by Buddha-Ghosha, who flourished about the beginning of the fifth century A.D., from the Siñhalese commentaries of Mahindo, an inspired follower of Gautama, and son of the king Aśoka.

Unlike the inflexible Brâhmaṇs—who, although diffusing their influence by self-renunciation and religious austerities that bore silent witness to the creed and worship of their forefathers, could not propagate their religion except by making Śûdras of all people whom they vanquished, believing that the spread of the higher elements of their religious knowledge among those who were not genuine Âryans was peculiarly profane—the Buddhists made no distinction in the quality of

* *S'ramana* is derived from the Sanskrit root *śram*, to work hard, and *Saman* from *sam*, to quiet.

† Dr. E. Roer's *Review of E. Burnouf's L'Histoire du Buddhisme Indien*, *Jour. As. Soc. Beng.* vol. xiv., pt. ii., p. 791, Calc. 1845.

persons they addressed; and in the synod of 246 B.C. a regular plan, analogous to that employed afterwards by Christian missionary societies, of translating Buddhist writings into foreign languages, along with pacific and persuasive teaching, was organized.

The language used in these early Indian scriptures seems to have been determined by geographical circumstances,—the Northern or the Nepâlese being written in Sanskṛit; the Southern or the Siñhalese in Pâli, the ancient language of the kingdom of Magadha, spoken by Śâkyamuni. From these two sources they have been translated into Tibetan, Mongol, Manchurian, Chinese, and also into several of the principal languages of Europe. From so many accessible fountains the knowledge of the moral precepts or apophthegms of Buddha, which for Oriental imagery, appropriate similes, and purity of ethics may vie successfully with those of any uninspired teacher of Egypt, Arabia, Greece, or Rome, was easily derived, and Buddhism marched forth in all its pristine vigour to subdue the kingdoms of the Eastern world. To mention only a few:—

"As a man elevated upon a mountain surveys in calmness the plains below, so does the virtuous man behold without emotion the struggles of the sinful multitude."

"As the solid rock stands unshaken by the storm, so the wise man is unmoved by contempt or applause."

"All the religion of Buddha is contained in these three sentences—purify the mind, abstain from vice, and practise virtue."

Although Buddha proclaimed the absolute equality of mankind, irrespective of caste, and the preëminence of virtue over all other worldly distinctions, he substituted nevertheless for the abolition of Brahmanical hierarchy his own vast *vihâras*, where monastic asceticism began soon to claim a high place in Indian society.

The doctrine of transmigration was not new to India; the Brâhmaṇs had equally believed in the inevitableness of change and decay, in the distribution of rewards and punishments, and the necessity of escaping the varying conditions of existence by absorption into the one and undivided Brahma,* but up to this time it had been a mere philosophical speculation. It was reserved for Śâkyamuni to convert this speculation into a religion. This religion rested upon an *opinion* admitted as a fact, and upon a *hope* presented as a certainty. The opinion was that in this world we see nothing but endless pain and misery; that all that is born

* *Bijdrage tot de Kennis van den Vedanta*, van A. Bruining: Leiden, 1870.

suffers pain, and that it is necessary to liberate ourselves from it. The hope was that knowledge and meditation alone offer the means of deliverance from corporeal and earthly existence. His teaching was both ideal and real: the ideal was that upon which he founded his pretensions to be a Buddha; the real was his own exemplary conduct. The spirit of gentleness and love, which pervaded it, had the effect of softening the manners of the people, and healing those angry feuds that had rent asunder the various kingdoms of India, as its extremely flexible and accommodating character that of becoming easily amalgamated with indigenous local superstitions of every description in the different countries it overspread; and it is no wonder that it very soon found favour and propagated itself with rapidity, not only throughout this country, but it moreover went far to transform the fierce nomads and wild savages of Central Asia into semi-civilized and comparatively virtuous men. As an instance of its extreme flexibility we may mention in passing that the Tibetan Buddhism displays the extravagancies of several Buddhist saints with horns in the forehead and a multiplicity of arms and faces—a morphology that is exceedingly repugnant to the more orthodox Buddhism of the South.

Śâkyamuni is certainly the oldest preacher in India, if not in the world, who, spurning the use of might, and by the mere force of precept and example, worked a pacific revolution in the thoughts of the Indians, and deposed quietly from its ancestral throne the proud theocracy of the orthodox Brâhmaṇs. Before the disciples of Thales of Miletus and his Ionian school had commenced to pursue their labours of cosmological dualism, and even long before Pythagoras had taught his doctrine of metempsychosis or founded his colony of philosophers in Græcia Magna, and the philosophical movements of the Eleatic schools were initiated, or Sophists born to confound the world with their metaphysical subtleties, the sage of Kapilavastu had already founded a philosophical school and created a religious sect, a sect that was in later times destined to embrace in its fold nearly four hundred millions of the faithful of different races and countries.

Notwithstanding the sublimity of his doctrine, however, the religion of Buddha is vague after all, and could not be better symbolized by its followers than by the *chakra* or wheel; for Gautama ignored the beginning and was equally uncertain as to the future. Fair, humane, and lovely as may be its outward forms, its inherent principles confessing no supreme God, its moral code void of all authorities, denying the true dignity and freedom of the human agent, and investing moral sentiments and relations with a kind of physical outsidedness, it has left the countries it has overrun a prey at once to superstition, political misrule, and spiritual lethargy. * His doctrine is a moving circle of uninterrupted pain, which even death does not put an end to; for transmigration is eternally waiting to punish in ugly shapes, besides the punition of the unceasing agony of existence itself, the man who was so unfortunate as not to succeed in gaining the merit of a Buddha, or attaining that undefined *nirvâṇa*, the *summum bonum* of the Buddhistic faith. Such belief is but a pessimistic resignation, a hypercritical contempt of the world, a state of hopelessness and of constant meditation on the woes of mankind, for which the mysterious, the incomprehensible nihilism or beatitude of *nirvâṇa* is, after all, a very poor compensation.

Some writers hold that Buddhism is essentially a code of practical morality, the so-called metaphysical and social philosophy having grown out of it in course of ages. This assertion is met by another from the veteran Lassen, who, with most Indianists, recognizes Buddhism to be a mere development of Kapila's Sânkhya, or, more precisely, the extension and practical embodiment of this rational or numeral system, as it is called.† The question admits of easy solution. Although one's experiences of Buddhist life may convince him that Gautama Buddha's is a practical code of morality without any philosophic system attached to it, it is to be observed that practically in India there is scarcely a code of morals or a system of religious doctrine without its cognate system of speculative philosophy. We are told by his biographers that Kapila's Sânkhya was a favourite study of Gautama Buddha, and he did evidently adopt the principles of the Sânkhya system—nay, he improved it. Kapila starts with the objects of our perceptions and sensation, and may therefore be considered materialistic. It teaches in fact the eternity of matter, and presses God, he thinks, between the horns of a dilemma. God, the philosopher tells us, could not create the universe without desire, and consequent want of power; for if he had desire, he could not have power; if power, he could not have desire. Again, *Prakṛiti*,—which

* "Chose étrange! Ceux qui méditent sur ces belles pages au lieu de conclure qu'il a une autre vie, où l'âme humaine doit trouver la satisfaction de ses immenses désirs, se retirent dans une négation désespéré."—Pavie, *Revue des Deux Mondes*, 1854, tome iv., p. 133.

† Lassen, *Ind. Alt.*, vol. i., pp. 830-831; Saint-Hilaire, *Des Vedas*, p. 147.

corresponds very much with matter, as explained by the most advanced school of modern materialists,—the rootless root, is the eternal cause of all things, and contains within itself 'the promise and potency' of all existing objects of whatever description and form. This is the inanimate and non-sentient principle, the intelligent and sentient counterpart of which is *Purusha*. The association of soul with matter is the cause of evil, and the cessation of evil the supreme end of soul. Freedom from the bondage of *Prakṛiti*, or the emancipation of soul, can only be obtained through knowledge. This is but the *Mukti* of the Sânkhya and the *Nirvâṇa* of the Buddhist, the difference being that the former places the supreme felicity of man in the complete cessation of all experience, whereas the latter goes a step beyond, and places it in the cessation not only of all experience, but of the experiencer also. The difference is one of degree, not of kind, and militates evidently in favour of Lassen's hypothesis that one doctrine is derived from the other.* Another notable difference is that while the Sânkhya denies God, but not the authority of the Vedas, and that, in spite of its sceptical tendency and the merciless logic with which many antiquated and contemporaneous errors were swept away, the authority of the Vedas is considered to have set the limits beyond which it would be simple rashness for thought to cross over; Gautama Buddha, on the contrary, takes the decisive step from which Kapila had recoiled. He denies the authority of the Vedas, and with it caste, sacrifice, superstition, sacerdotal oligarchy and despotism. Kapila struck at the root of the authority of the Vedas, and at the same time displayed a real or pretended reverence for them. Śâkyamuni accepted the logic but rejected the conclusion. Such are then the doctrines of a system to which Buddhism stands in the obvious relation of offspring to parent.

Regarding the comparative antiquity of Brahmanism and Buddhism, it has been put forth as an argument that most of the epigraphic monuments in India are all of the Buddhistic, and not of the Brahmanical worship, or that the architectural evidence is almost all on the side of the antiquity of Buddhism, and that similar evidences of the religion of the Brâhmaṇs hardly exist. But this is exactly what proves the priority of Brahmanism to Buddhism, as that of Judaism to Christianity.

* For details of Kapila's system see Dr. Ballantyne's *Aphorisms of Kapila*, and *Lectures on the Sankhya Philosophy*, Mirzapore, 1850; Colebrooke and Wilson, *Miscellaneous Works*; Max Müller's *Chips from a German Workshop*; *Kusumanjali*, &c.

By comparing, likewise, the Buddhaic monachism with the ascetic life of the Brâhmaṇs, certain relations are elicited which prove the latter to have preceded the former. These relations may well be likened to those subsisting between the patriarchal and municipal *régimes* of the primitive human society.

The sacerdotal life of the Brâhmaṇ had four distinct stages: in the first he was a student and a servant of his preceptor; in the second he married and lived with his family, though engaged all the while in teaching the Vedas; in the third he withdrew himself into some mountain fastness to spend his life as a solitaire, his body covered with the bark of trees, and his sustenance consisting of roots and leaves of plants; in the fourth, absorbed in the contemplation of the Almighty and truth, freed from all the trammels of the world, his nature subdued, and his passions silenced, his soul was only too glad to quit the earth. Gautama Buddha, however, introduced four very remarkable modifications in the mendicant order of his followers, planned as they were at first on the same Brahmanical type. He admittted no gradations. The moment a Buddhist novice entered the monastery, he was believed to have broken off all the ties of kinship, and did not think of leaving the monastery again. While the Brâhmaṇ spent his life in laborious study, tuition, austerities, retirement and self-denial, one stage of which allowed him the fruition of all the secular privileges of a layman, the Buddhist Bhikśuka, like the Christian monk, having once made his ingress into a religious order, could hardly ever think of returning to the society of his friends. The Brâhmaṇ by the right of his birth had conferred on him almost divine prerogatives to be transmitted to his posterity, and was often both a possessor of riches and had numerous offspring to share his patrimony; the Buddhist, on the contrary, made his position in the world depend entirely upon his individual merit, a few yellow pieces of raiment were his clothes, a dark cell in the *vihâra* his permanent habitation, and an alms-pot all his chattels.

Thus while we hold that the foundation of monastic corporations by Gautama Buddha was chronologically posterior to the institution of the sacerdotal charge of the Brâhmaṇs, we must at the same time discredit the divergence the Buddhist mendicancy gave rise to being any step in advance of the Brahmanical asceticism. Although the austere life led by the Buddhist monks went far to win the admiration of some Christian Fathers, and to recommend the system to St. Basil, who inaugurated on this Oriental model his own large religious communities, it was not long before the evil resulting from the abuse of meditation and of idleness on the Buddhaic type was detected and remedied. While princes, whom the feudal system gave, as the lords of the soil, a right of service from the holders, but who in the transfer of lands to monastic bodies had become deprived of this privilege, were framing laws, *e. g.* the *Statute of Mortmain* of Edward II. of England in 1279, to prohibit these bodies from getting more in this way, some prudent ecclesiastics, especially St. Benedict, to save their cenobites from falling into sloth and moral oscitancy, were imposing on them rules to lead a more active life, work with their own hands, and establishing convocations to enable the clergy to tax themselves.*

The history and actual observation of both the social and political organizations of the two religions prove, moreover, that the *Sûtras* were coetaneous with an epoch when the Vedas and the Puranic legends formed the foundation of religious belief in India, and which really paved the way for their advent. The abstract form of Buddhism displays it as a natural growth from, or reaction against, Brahmanism, whose material and elemental worship is in striking contrast with the knowledge of the physical and moral laws possessed by the Buddhist, who, to be a member of the militant church, had to practise the six transcendental perfections, viz. alms, morals, science, energy, patience, and charity. Buddhism is distinguished, besides, as being genetically posterior to Brahmanism, or an advance upon a primitive stage of religious thought, from the fact of the former believing the practice of morality to be the supreme law, or at least evincing a decided predilection for moral sentiments, which occupy so conspicuous a place in that creed, while the latter is fond of ontological theories and mythology, which is but a lower stage of religious life in the scale of humanity. †

The monuments are, assuredly, a rich mine of information, which, when duly explored, will yet clear up, I trust, many doubts concerning the life and relics of Buddha ; they are in fact what Mr. Fergusson so

---

* *Revue des deux Mondes*, 1er Novembre 1854, 1er Mars, 1860.

† As from the school of Kapila to that of Buddha the transition, as above mentioned, is obvious and direct, some writers think that a similar parallel may be established between the school of Buddha and the Vedânta, which followed in the wake of declining Buddhism. For a comparison of Essenism, Mahomedanism, and Buddhism the reader may consult with advantage Hardwick's *Christ and other Masters*, Wheeler's *History of India*, and *The Academy*, 1875, p. 161.

appropriately terms them, "the pictorial bible of Buddhism,"—for, the epigraphic documents abounding in the friezes and bas-reliefs of Buddhistic monuments, in the sculptures on the gateways of Sânchi, and the Topes of Amarâvatî, in the frescoes of Ajaṇṭâ, and in the inscriptions in the naves of the Kanheri and Nâsik caves, and other architectural relics and statuary to be found throughout India, are really marvellous archæological repertories of Buddhistic legendary history; but this does not for certain militate against the antiquity of the Vedantic school. Far advanced in philosophical speculations and didactic subtleties, the Brâhmaṇs, professing the simple monotheism of the Vedas and of the Institutes of Manu, which led to a kind of household religion, retained, like the Patriarchs of the Old Testament, the simple spirit of native worship, or, more like the modern Arabs of the desert, worshipped God in the open air, employing but the most modest, if not rude, altars for their sacrifices, their burnt-offerings of clarified butter, and their libations of *soma* liquor. This accounts then for the fact of our not possessing any architectural monuments previous to Buddhism.

Śâkya's doctrine—so sublime, so spiritual, insinuating into one's mind the belief that man's supreme destiny is deliverance from the trammels of this wicked world, and notable for the establishment of mutual connection and brotherhood among his followers by those beautiful *vihâras*, enormous temples excavated from the living rock, or monastic institutions intended as much to be asylums for the religious as places of repose for travelling ascetics and foreigners, breathing forth a spirit of charity that only as late as the mediæval times did civilized Europe try to imitate and propagate—an organization of the Buddhist militia, whose wonderful exertions can only be likened in the world to the great efforts put forth by the disciples of Loyola during the nascent period of that great order, and whose extraordinary resemblance is moreover heightened by the fact that both employed only celibates as their agents—was at last destined to undergo a painful ordeal, a humiliating probation. Having once truly realized the ideal of Buddhism in the pastoral beauty in which they were first founded, having lived in happy simplicity and innocent communion as moral regenerators of mankind, these *vihâras* or hermitages became in process of time extensive land-owners, absorbing a great portion of the soil into mortmain,—so flourishing, in the popular or mundane sense of the word, that they degenerated into the very hotbeds of intrigue and chicanery, engendering desires of honours, opulence, and ambition, and raising adversaries amidst the very persons who were bound to be its patrons. Thus the very strength of Buddhism—its legions of unmarried monks—became its weakest point. The inmates of these mountain caves quitting active duty and taking refuge in lazy isolation, destructive to one's affections, and which made them more illiberal and dangerous to independence of thought than their not so well disciplined and less aggressive but more freehearted antagonists, the Bráhmaṇs, were actuated by motives political rather than spiritual. The admirable code of morality and the grand principles of truly human charity and compassion taught by the illustrious founder of their monachism was set aside, the spirit of gentleness and an ardent desire to make others virtuous, courtesy to strangers, social hospitality, and toleration without restraint, that once distinguished most of its professors, sacrificed for their temporal welfare, and the austerities of the Buddhist monk that once far surpassed those of the stigmatized disciples of St. Francis, and the habit of contemplation that was carried to an extent that has not been equalled in the history of the world, exchanged for mere ceremonial observances and ease. But this state of things must have been preceded by conflicts of metaphysical speculations, and of schisms and heresies in Buddha's doctrine.

The phases of evolution the Buddhistic doctrine has gone through may be classified into three, viz. sceptical, traditionary, and ultra-superstitious, as three are also the principal philosophical schools it gave rise to formerly, to be revived only in later times, in modern Europe. One school admits no other existence than that of mind or spirit, an existence revealed in reflection. This is a system of spiritualism and idealism. It resembles the philosophical opinions of Berkeley. The second, in opposition to the first, professes sensualism and materialism, divided into two sections: one holding that the senses perceive external objects immediately, and that it is by induction we conclude the existence of elements which compose these objects; the other that the senses do not perceive external objects immediately, but only by means of images. The principles of their system coincide in many points with the materialism of Cabanis. The third, surpassing all bounds of former negations, teaches that there exists nothing real except the eternal *self*. This is an individual pantheism, in opposition to other pantheistic systems in which all individualities are merely phenomenal. This may well be considered as the source from which the individual pantheism of Fichte is derived.

The religious sects also had their different characteristics, which have up to the present remained unchanged. One professes the doctrine of the *Hînayâna* or 'Small Vehicle,' which is, like our primitive church, more ancient in ritual and liturgy, and has always remained faithful to her primordial simplicity. It numbers among its proselytes the nations of the south and west of Asia, who employ in their prayers, as before noted, the ancient dialect of Magadha. The other is the *Mahâyâna* or 'Great Vehicle,' which is but a renovation of Buddha's doctrine, or rather a new revolution, made about five centuries after Buddha's death, and whose author is Nâgârjuṇa. It has propagated itself among the peoples towards the north of Asia, whose scriptures are principally written in Sanskṛit. This latter sect resembles Roman Catholicism in many respects; it has not only monasteries for men and women, mendicancy practised as a religious virtue, celibacy and tonsure of its monks, bells and chaplets; but also the worship of relics, auricular confession, intercession of saints, fasts, processions, litanies, and holy water. To make the resemblance more perfect, there is in Tibet a hierarchy of Grand Lamas, the cardinals of the Buddhistic Church, with a cross, mitre, and dalmatic for their insignia, and the *Tale-Lama* at their head, who is elected by a conclave, and represents on earth the true vicar of Buddha.*

Few remains of ancient India appeal more forcibly to the imagination, or are more suggestive of departed greatness, than the various religious monuments erected by Buddhism, amongst which are particularly to be mentioned the *vihâras, stûpas, dâgobâs*, and *chaityas*. *Vihâra* caves are monasteries containing *gṛihas* or cells, generally square in form, supported by rows of pillars either running round them and separating the great central *shâlâ* or hall from the aisles, or disposed in four equidistant lines. *Stûpas* or *topes* are solid hemispherical buildings, varying in size from the great Sânchi Tope, which is 106 feet in diameter, to the smallest at Bhojpur, which is only 6 feet in diameter. I say hemispherical because the primordial topes were so, but those next in antiquity were raised a few feet above the plinth by the addition of a cylindrical portion; while another class, such as the Sarnâth Tope near Benares, had the hemisphere raised to a

* Father Bury, a Catholic missionary in China, on beholding the bonzes dressed as himself, tonsured, using rosaries, &c., exclaimed—"There is not a piece of dress, not a sacerdotal function, not a ceremony of the Church of Rome which the devil has not invented a copy of in this country."—Kerson, *The Cross and the Dragon*, p. 185, Lond. 1854. See also Quinet, *Génie des Religions*, pp. 251 *et seq.*: Paris, 1857.

height equal to its own diameter. Their great size obtained for them the designation of the Indian Pyramids, in contradistinction to the Egyptian and Babylonian pyramids; but, unlike the majestic productions of the Egyptian architects, the Indian *stûpas* have a ponderous and ignoble appearance. While the purposes for which the pyramids were intended are yet unknown, all conjectures amounting to the expression that they were designed for astronomical and religious purposes, *stûpas* are mostly sepulchral, and a few are religious edifices dedicated either to the celestial Âdi Buddha, the great first cause of all things, or to one of his emanations, the *Manushi* or mortal Buddhas, of whom Śâkyamuni is the last. The shape of the *stûpas* is said to be derived from a legend that Buddha was wont to compare life to a water-bubble. They are the *chortens* of the Tibetans, and chronologically are posterior to the *vihâras*, most of them being probably erected during the period commencing with the first years of the Christian era, and terminating in the sixth century.* *Dâgobâ* (written also *dahgoba, daghopa* or *dehgop*) is derived from the Sanskṛit *deh*, 'the body,' and *gup*, to hide, or from *dhâtugarbha*, 'the holder' of a relic or elementary principle. They seem meant for cenotaphs, in imitation of the monumental receptacles built over the relics of the Buddhas and the Bodhisatvas. *Chaitya* is a place of worship, within the circular end of the nave of which stands the *dâgobâ*.

It is a trite saying that mankind from its earliest days, long before writing materials were invented, was in the habit of expressing its grandest conceptions and noblest sentiments in architectural monuments. This ancient idea of the dawn of civilization has been transmitted to modern nations, who vie with one another in embodying in the magnitude of their public buildings their great thoughts and national feelings. England expresses her religious feeling by her St. Paul's Cathedral, as the Pantheon the admiration for their distinguished countrymen among the French, and the Capitol of Washington the love of liberty among the Americans. The Buddhist India has also embodied in her *stûpas* and *dâgobâs* her highest regard for the great sage and the Bodhisatvas.

In less than two centuries from the decease of Buddha, the system he established had spread throughout the whole of India, overcoming

* For details see Ritter, *Die Stupas*, Berlin, 1854; Wilson, *Ariana Antiqua*, Lond. 1841; Emil Schlagintweit, *Buddhism in Tibet*, Leipzig, 1863; Cunningham, *Bhilsa Topes*, 1854; and *Opening of the Topes*, &c., *Jour. R. As. Soc.* vol. ix., p. 108.

opposition the most formidable, and binding together the most discordant elements; nay, it went far into distant lands, where a sort of geniolatry, similar to that we see now existing among various half-civilized tribes of Africa and Polynesia, was preparing a genial soil for the deposition of the seed of Buddhism to grow up soon after luxuriantly, without meeting any serious hindrance to check its growth. The changes Buddhism had undergone were most remarkable. Having driven the hierarchy of caste from its stronghold, having overcome the religion of the Brâhmaṇs on its own ground and seized by its kings the greater part of India, its scriptures are forgotten * except by its corrupt sectaries, the compromising half-polytheistic half-pantheistic Jainas; its original sources of the Sanskṛit and Pâli literature entirely neglected,—all the information being derived from the secondary sources of the Burmese, Mongol and Chinese, and the once philosophic and religious doctrines that did for the civilization of Central and Western Asia what Christianity has done for the barbarians of Europe rendered monstrous by the admixture of extravagant myths and traditions. Thus the worship of Buddhism, from its being simple and attractive, without many dogmas and rites, its religious ceremonies consisting in the offering of flowers and perfumes accompanied with the recital of hymns and pious prayers, had at last retrograded to that of not only the representation of the figure of Śâkyamuni, but of *dâgobâs* or bell-shaped mounds enshrining a part of his bones, hair, or his tooth—in fact, of his whole *śarira* (body)—being held up as the true object of the Buddhist adoration, besides the trees, the *nâgas* or many-headed men-serpents, the Gandharvas and Kinnaras—human-headed birds and horse-faced beings—and the other *dii minores* of the Buddhistic pantheon.†

---

* In the eleventh century Buddhism was confined to a few localities, and in the sixteenth, when Abulfazl, the minister of Akbar, was exploring the characteristics of all religions, he could find no one to enlighten him respecting Buddhism.

† The Eastern Peninsula is, however, an exception to this state of retrogression. My friend Dr. Oliver Codrington, Honorary Secretary of the Bombay Branch of the Royal Asiatic Society, to whom I am much indebted for kind help and valuable suggestions in the course of my researches bearing on the subject, and who has personal experience of the Burmese, informs me that they still keep up their simplicity of worship, and are regularly instructed in Pâli books. Bishop Bigandet says:—"Owing to its geographical position, and perhaps also to political causes, Burmah has ever remained out of the reach of the Hindu influence, which in Nepâl has coloured Buddhism with Hindu myths and habited it in gross *idolatric* forms."—*The Life or Legend of Gaudama*, Rangoon, 1866, pp. viii.-ix.

History indeed repeats itself. What Śâkyamuni once did in India Francesco d'Assisi repeated in Italy. And confronting the two peninsulas, that exhibit so many points of affinity in their physical and social organization, what a singular contrast does one bear towards the other! While one presents all the symptoms of a rising nation, springing, as it were, like the Phœnix of the fable, from its own ashes, the other is but a vast catacomb of a dead civilization, that, in the elegant phrase of Michelet, "en son berceau originaire fut la matrice du monde, la principale et dominante source de races, des idées, et des langues, pour la Grèce et Rome, l'Europe moderne.*

The Italian preacher of the Middle Ages left, like Śâkya, an affluent position to become a solitary and a mendicant, drew numbers of disciples after him, established his own organization in counterpoise to that of the feudal system, gave to the Śûdras and the Chaṇḍâlas of Europe in the Church, that had reverted to the old system of castes, as free admittance as to the privileged classes; and his amiable character was as sweetly sung by Dante as that of the great Gautama by Dhammakitti Thera, and the Italian painters loved to represent him, just as well as the sculptors of Bhilsa, Amarâvatì, and Ajaṇṭâ loved to chisel the image of Buddha. His Tertiaries interpret as faithfully the mission of their pious founder as the *vihâras* that of Śâkyamuni. The former passed away most naturally when the want ceased, or only decayed in time; the latter was suppressed before attaining its full maturity,—was almost stifled in the cradle.

Crusades were inaugurated for the suppression of Buddhism. Two great causes, the one moral, the other social, led India into them. The moral cause was the impulse derived from religious sentiments, and ever fomented by the preaching of Kumarila, Śaṅkarâchârya, and other revivalists of modern Vedantism. Śaṅkarâchârya, the principal teacher of Śaivaism, a native of the Mâlayalam country, who flourished about the eighth century of the Christian era, was travelling far and wide as a polemic to preach crusades against Buddhism, which, unlike the Christian crusades, which failed in the principal object of rescuing the Holy Sepulchre from the hands of the Saracen followers of Mahomed and expelling them from the birthplace of Christianity, terminated in the culminating crisis of expelling that faith from its holy land. The theatre of this mighty contest was more

* *Bible de l'Humanité*, Troisième édition, Paris, 1864, p. 15.

southern than Gangetic India, the Galilee of Buddhism. It was a religious war, attended with its *cortège* of horrors, of carnage and devastation. The 37th sloka of the first chapter of the *Śaṅkara-vijaya* describes the Kâpâlas, an order of Buddhist monks who prowled about naked in the streets, carrying a human skull in their hands and practising horrid rites, the principal of which was to victimize the Brâhmaṇs and those who had seceded from the Buddhist church. In the *Bhâgavat*, on the other hand, it is declared that at the commencement of the Kâliyuga, Vishṇu became incarnate in Kitâka, another name of Buddha, for the purpose of deluding the enemies of the gods. The same legend is related more in detail in the *Kashi Khaṇḍa* of the *Skanda Purâṇa*, and also in the *Ganeśa-Upa-Purâṇa*, where Buddha is described more as one of the emanations of Brahma than as an *avatâr* of Vishṇu, and as the deliverer of the Daityas, Danavas, and other heretics. Among the Brahmanical imprecations there is one in the *Kalpalatikâ* in which the Brâhmaṇs vow to fill "all the lakes of India with the blood of the Buddhists."

Another cause, the social state of India in the seventh century, equally contributed to the breaking forth of these crusades. This I have already explained. The Buddhist society, its rich prelates and monks, the official Buddhism fed by gifts of the rich and feared by the poor, after exchanging for the religion of the heart mere outward observances, had become an utterly obnoxious institution in the country by its overweening demeanour and arrogant impositions. But it was not until about the twelfth century of our era that Buddhism was entirely extirpated from India, as in the *Mâdhavavijaya*, ch. v., śl. 16, we are told of Buddhists preaching against modern Vedantism in the Śaivite or Vaishṇavite manifestation, especially of the celebrated Vadisinu or Budhisâgara, who held a long disputation with the founder of Vaishnavism, the famous reformer Mâdhavachârya, and was at last defeated in argument. We cannot say, however, that Buddhism was completely eradicated from India, for as Buddhism had its roots in Brahmanism, and principally in the Sânkhya, and Brahmanism in an earlier religion—the worship of the elements, especially the one generally called the Sabæan or Mithraic faith—so not only Jainism, but both Śaivism and Vaishṇavism, had their roots in Buddhism. Only a comparative study of them all together can show us affinities and differences. This task remains yet to be done, in spite of all the great but not undetached researches of Colebrooke, Wilson, and others.

The illustrious Śâkya is principally worshipped in his relics, which according to tradition were collected on the funeral pile of the great Gautama, and then enclosed in eight metallic cylinders, over which were raised the same number of churches (*chaityas*), whose primitive timber frames eventually grew into gigantic mausoleums. The worship of relics was the earliest innovation on the original simplicity of the Buddhist religion.

These relics are innumerable; they seem to have reproduced themselves or multiplied *ad infinitum* in process of time. Pandora's box probably did not contain so many divine gifts as the *vihâras*, *dâgobâs*, *stûpas*, and *chaityas* are said to hold. They range from fragments of Buddha's body to memorials of his begging life, and other objects associated with scenes in his career; from the frontal and collar bones to the ashes of his body, the latter interred along the corner-stone of every Buddhist temple. Their distribution seems to have proceeded on homœopathic measure; for the quantities given out must have really been infinitesimal. A lock of his hair and his left collar-bone are said to be buried under Mahiyangana Dâgobâ; eight of his hairs under the great pagoda of Rangoon; his right collar-bone, the dish from which he usually ate, and some of the ashes of his body, under Thupârâma Dâgobâ in Anurâdhapura; one-eighth of the ashes under the Ruwanvæli Dâgobâ in the same city; besides a minute portion of the ashes under the dâgobâ of almost every Buddhist chaitya in Ceylon and elsewhere. Other objects are his alms-bowl; the tree under which he sat at Gaya—to be described hereafter; the waterpot at Candahar, which however, like the footprint of Ceylon, the Mahomedans have usurped, changing of course its designation, as belonging to their saint Ali. The waterpot is made of stone, and is said to hold twenty gallons. Hiwen Thsang says he visited two places where Buddha was said to have left his luminous shadow, but that in later ages they had only a doubtful and feeble resemblance.*

* Respecting Buddha's relics the *Dhâtuvanśa's* description is rather interesting, and I cannot forbear quoting it *verbatim*. To commence with the ceremony of the cremation of the mortal remains of the Hindu sage:—

"46. Thereafter, by the power of the gods, fire was kindled in the pile; there was neither soot nor ashes of the body of the Teacher when burnt.

"47. By the will of Buddha there remained relics of the colour of pearls and of the lustre of gold scattered in various ways.

The relics of the disciples of Buddha are also preserved with reverent care, and in Ceylon those of the great apostle Mahindo, the Buddhist St. Augustine, share with the tooth of his master the homage of worshippers. Now as regards Buddha's teeth they are so numerous that, considering he died at the advanced age of eighty-one, it is scarcely probable he should have preserved them all, although it is not rare to see in octogenarians in this country the maxillary apparatus as perfect as in a man of thirty. Be this, however, as it may, it is an ascertained fact that four at least of the great Indian reformer's teeth are historically held to be his relics, viz. the one at Weruwawela in Ceylon, which strangely has obtained little or no reputation; another at Amarâpurâ in Burmah, which seems to have somehow been tampered with, nothing having been said in explanation of its sudden absence; a third in the possession of the Tartars; and the last, the most celebrated of all, is the *dalada* or tooth-relic of Ceylon.

"48. These seven relics, the bone of the forehead, the two collar-bones, (and) the four tooth-relics of Buddha, were not dispersed.

"49. Streams of water descending from the skies, and rising from the earth on all sides, extinguished the fire of the pile.

"50. The priest named Sarabhû, the disciple of the priest Sâripatta, who was endowed with supernatural power, (and) had attained the fourfold knowledge,

"51. Having removed the neck-relic from the funeral pile, placed it in the Thûpa at Mahiyangana (and) made a monument encasing it.

"52. The sage called Khema, possessed of kindness, (and) freed from Saññojana, took there the left tooth-relic from the funeral pile.

"53. There the eminent Brâhman Dona, appeasing the quarrel which rose amongst eight kings on account of relics of Buddha,

"54. (And) dividing the remaining relics, made them into eight portions (and) gave them to eight kings living in different cities.

"55. The kings, exceedingly joyful, received those relics, (and,) departing, built monuments (for them), each in his own country.

"56. One relic was honoured and worshipped by Sakka, one by the inhabitants of Gandhâra, one by the Nága kings.

"57. Then Khema gave the tooth-relic taken by him to Brahmadatta, king of Kalinga, in Dantapura."

MEMOIR ON THE HISTORY OF THE TOOTH-RELIC OF CEYLON.

The field hitherto explored of Śâkyamuni's philosophy being already so wide, and the domain of Buddhistic literature so extensive, it appears surprising that so interesting a subject as the Tooth-relic of Gautama Buddha, with its romantic wanderings and adventures, should so seldom be alluded to. It is only the ancient *vaṅśas* or classical chronicles of Ceylon and of the kingdoms of the Malay Peninsula, and books chiefly descriptive or historical of those countries, that contain some meagre accounts of the tooth-relic, so thinly scattered among a large mass of other topics that not unfrequently they are entirely overlooked.

There is no lack of arguments, however, to justify this neglect, the principal being the absolute want until lately of trustworthy and complete translations of the ancient Buddhist annals into modern languages, especially the two most familiar in Europe—the French and the English*—and the spirit of the marvellous, so characteristic of the infancy of civilization, predominating amongst them, and producing an admixture of the fantastic with the real, so fatal to the rigidness and severity of historical truth, and totally repugnant to the stoical lover of dates and facts.

It is well known that while tradition and documentary evidence are by one party pressed forward in support of the statement that the so-called *Dalada* or tooth-relic of Buddha was captured and destroyed by the Portuguese in the sixteenth century A.D., it is contended by the other that it is still preserved in the Maligâva temple at Kandy, as fresh as when it was first rescued by Khema from the great teacher's funeral pyre in Kuśinagara,† about twenty-five centuries ago.

* "Qui veut arriver à un grand public doit aujourd'hui écrire en anglais ou en français."—Edouard Laboulaye, *Dis. Prelim.* Vassilief's *Bouddisme,* Paris, 1865, p. xvi.

† Kuśinagara, the scene of Buddha's *nirvâna*, has been identified with Kâśiâ, about 110 miles N.NE. of Benares. It is believed that the very spot marked in ancient times by a reclining figure, representing Buddha in the attitude in which he died, may now be recognized in the site of the *stûpa* or heap of ruins the name of which is translated as "the foot of the dead prince," while the spot where his body was burned would correspond with the site of the *great stûpa* called *Devisthân.*—Cunningham's *Ancient Geography of India,* pp. 431, 432; Alabaster's *Wheel of the Law,* p. 165.

Both statements, so diametrically opposed, cannot of course be correct.

Partly from a desire to collect all the available information that may serve to throw light on the subject, especially from the Portuguese annalists of the period and their European contemporaries, and partly from the interest and curiosity I, with several others, feel in all that concerns the venerable Hindu sage, this attempt at one connected and continuous narrative has been made.

The earliest authentic records of this tooth-relic of Buddha are—FIRST, the *Daladâvaṅśa* or *Dhâtâdhâtuvaṅśa,* contracted into *Dhâtuvaṅśa* or Chronicle of the Tooth, of unknown authorship, written formerly in Elu, the ancient language of the Sihalese, about the year 310 A.D., and translated into Pâli by the priest Dhammakitti Thera in the thirteenth century A.D.* SECONDLY, the *Mahâvaṅśa,* a metrical chronicle, which literally means 'the Genealogy of the Great,' containing the early history of the kings *Mahavaṅśe,* or the Great Dynasty, of Ceylon. The first section of this Odyssey of the Siñhalese, extending from 543 B.C. to 301 A.D., was compiled in the reign of his nephew, the king Datusena, between the years 459 and 477 A.D., by the priest Mahânamo, and is based both on the *Dîpavaṅśa*—a work of greater antiquity but yet of unknown authorship, which unfortunately ends just before the events recorded in the *Dhâtuvaṅśa* took place—and on annals in the vernacular language then existing at Anuradhâpura, the ancient capital of Ceylon. The second section was written in the reign of the *Saluvaṅśe,* or the Inferior Dynasty, the story of whose line occupies the continuation of this mystic chronicle. It was the king Paṇḍita Parakrâma Bâhu III. who caused it, under orders of another illustrious king of the same name, to be extended as far as the year 1266 A.D.; and thence the narrative has been carried on, under subsequent sovereigns, down to the year 1758 A.D., the latest chapters being compiled by command of Kṛiti Śrî, the king of Kandy, partly from Siñhalese works brought back from Siam, and partly from native historical accounts preserved from the general destruction decreed about the year 1590 A.D. by the apostate from Buddhism, Râja Siñha I. It is the second section that alludes to the history of the tooth. THIRDLY, the *Râjavali,* a work of different hands, compiled from local annals and used generally as a corol-

* According to Mr. D'Alwis the *Dathavaṅśa* appeared in 1326 A.D., but he gives no authority for this statement: *Introduction to Sidat Sangarâwa,* p. clxxv.

lary or addition to the *Mahâvaṅśa*,* as well as to the *Râjaratnâkarî*,—the latter also a valuable historical work, deservedly held in high estimation by the Buddhists as a record of events from 540 B.C. to the settlement of the Portuguese in the metropolis of their religion in India. The *Râjavali* continues the narration through the mighty struggle for political ascendancy between the Portuguese and their rivals the Dutch, which resulted in the latter gaining possession of Colombo, and ultimately of all the maritime districts of the island.† FOURTHLY, the *Phrâ Pâthom*, a Siamese version of a Pâli work partially translated by Colonel Low.‡

The *Dhâtuvaṅśa*, which, as chronicling the events connected with the tooth, is naturally regarded as the great authority on the subject, is said to have been written, as already mentioned, about 310 A.D., when the relic was first brought to Ceylon from Dantapura (Odontopolis) in Kaliṅga, in Southern India.§ The original work in Elu is said to have experienced the fate that befell all the Siṅhalese chronicles and commentaries during the reign of Parakrâma the Great's widow, Lilâvatî, who reigned as queen at Pollanarua three times, and was dethroned as often—in 1197-1200, 1209-10, and again in 1211-12 A.D.—that of being entirely rewritten in Pâli, which unfortunately caused almost all the Elu works to disappear; although Turnour, well known as the Colebrooke of the Siṅhalese *savants*, notes that it was still extant in Ceylon in 1837.‖ As regards the antiquity of the

* It is also said that ample allusion is made to the tooth-relic in several chapters of the untranslated portions of the *Mahâvaṅśa*.

† Upham's *Collection of Tracts*, &c., Lond. 1833. Burnouf's articles in the *Journal des Savants*, 1833 (Sept.), 1834 (Jan. and Apr.).

‡ *Jour. R. As. Soc. Beng.*, Cal. 1848, vol. xvii., pt. ii., p. 82.

§ The town of Dandagula, the Dantapura of the Buddhist chronicles, is now Râjamâhendri, which is about 30 miles to the north-east of Koriṅga: see Colonel Cunningham's *Ancient Geography of India*, pp. 518-19. Another Dantapura is said to have been situated on the northern bank of the Kṛishṇa, and to correspond with the modern Amaravati, one of the ancient Tri-Kaliṅgas.

‖ *Jour. As. Soc. Beng.*, Cal. 1837, vol. i., pp. 856 *et seq.* Turnour also supposes the tooth-relic of Ceylon to be alluded to in the opening passage of the *Firuz Lât* Inscription, but this has been questioned by later writers.

The inscription, facing west, is as follows:—"The Râja Pâṇḍu, who was the delight of the Devas, has thus said: 'This inscription on *Dhammo* is recorded by me in the twenty-seventh year of my inauguration. My public functionaries intermingle among many hundred thousands of living creatures, as well as human beings. If any one of them should inflict injuries on the most alien of these beings, what advantage would there be in this my edict? [On the other hand,] should these functionaries follow a line of conduct tending to allay alarm, they would confer prosperity and happiness on the people, as well as on the country; and by such a benevolent procedure they will acquire a know-

Dhâtuvaṅśa, to prove that it was really composed 310 A.D., or, at the latest, some time before the end of the fifth century of our era, an argument founded on this work being alluded to in the 37th chapter of the *Mahâvaṅśa*—which, as above stated, was compiled between 459 and 477 A.D.—has been put forth. In the *Mahâvaṅśa* the chronicle is referred to thus:—"In the ninth year of his reign Śrîmeghavana (or Meghavarṇa, possibly the Varâja of the Western Cave-Inscriptions—see *Jour. Bom. Br. R. As. Soc.*, vol. v., p. 42), a certain Brâhmaṇa princess brought the *Dhâtâdhâtu* or tooth-relic of Buddha hither from Kaliṅga, under the circumstances set forth in the *Dhâtâdhâtuvaṅśa.*" Now the *Mahâvaṅśa*, notwithstanding its accepted authenticity and chronological precision, was not completed, as before mentioned, between 459 and 477 A.D. It contains a hundred chapters in all, divided into sections, and only its first section, compiled within that interval, extends to 301 A.D. or the end of Mahâsena's reign, while the *Dhâtuvaṅśa* is said to have been written when the relic was removed to Ceylon, in the ninth year of the reign of his successor, *i.e.* 310 A.D.

Difficult as it is, then, to assign a fixed date to its composition, concurrent circumstances, too tedious to enumerate here, have led

---

ledge of the condition both of the prosperous and of the wretched, and will at the same time prove to the people and the country that they have not departed from *Dhammo*. Why should they inflict an injury either on a countryman of their own or an alien? Should my functionaries act tyrannically, my people, loudly lamenting, will be appealing to me, and will appear also to have become alienated [from the effects of orders enforced] by royal authority. Those ministers of mine who proceed on circuits, so far from inflicting oppressions, should cherish the people as the infant in arms is cherished by the wet-nurse; and those experienced circuit ministers, moreover, like unto the wet-nurse, should watch over the welfare of my child (the people). By such a procedure my ministers would ensure perfect happiness to my realm.

"'By such a course, these (the people) released from all disquietude, and most fully conscious of their security, would devote themselves to their avocations. By the same procedure, on its being proclaimed that the grievous power of my ministers to inflict tortures is abolished, it would prove a worthy subject of joy, and be the established compact (law of the land). Let the criminal judges or executioners of sentences [in the instances] of persons committed to prison, or who are sentenced to undergo specific punishments, without my special sanction, continue their judicial investigations for three days, till my decision be given. Let them also, as regards the welfare of living creatures, attend to what affects their conservation, as well as their destruction; let them establish offerings; let them set aside animosity.

"'Hence those who observe and who act up to our precepts would abstain from afflicting another. To the people also many blessings will result by living in *Dhammo*. The merit resulting from the charity would spontaneously manifest itself.'"—Turnour on the Inscriptions on the Columns at Delhi, &c.

I quote these lines from the edition of the *Dhâtuvaṅśa* by Sir Swâmi, who, in respect to the inscription, says: "The spirit of universal charity and philanthropy which animates this draft is not unworthy of the consideration of the present enlightened rulers of the great Indian empire."—*Introd.*

scholars, like Turnour and others, to think that at least the first portion of it was written some time before the end of the 5th century of the Christian era, and that two sections were subsequently added to it, bringing the history of the *dalada* down to the middle of the eighteenth century.

Dhammakitti Thera, the author of the Pâli work—who among his other titles to eminence takes to himself that of a royal preceptor, and flourished in the thirteenth century of our era—has written a preface to his book,* in which he lays down the following reasons for undertaking the task of translating the *Daladâvaṅśa* from Elu:—(1) That the *Mahâvaṅśa*, merely referring to the *Daladâvaṅśa*, says scarcely anything about the relic; (2) that the *Daladâvaṅśa* is too long, being full of details about the death of Buddha and the history of the relic immediately after that event; and (3) that the Elu language, in which the *Daladâvaṅśa* is written, is hard for the Siṅhalese to understand. In the poem itself (ch. v., v. 10, of Sir Swâmi's edition), he adds a fourth, viz: "for the benefit of those who live in other lands." From this it is apparent that Thera not only translated, but even abridged, the original. It terminates just at the period of the arrival of the relic at Anurâdhapura, in Ceylon.† Of the translation Turnour was the first to give a brief analysis, in the *Journal of the Bengal Asiatic Society* in 1837, and it was only last year that a translation into English was published in London by Sir Swâmi. It is an excellent translation, so far as I am able to judge, but I cannot help concurring with Mr. Rhys Davids, who in a review of the work writes:—"It is to be regretted that the interesting history of the tooth has not been more thoroughly discussed in the Introduction." (*The Academy*, Sept. 1874, p. 341.)

Besides these there are other accounts of the relic, of secondary importance, but all bearing testimony to the devotional feeling, heroic achievements, magnificent designs, and bitter disappointments of which it has been the witness. There has probably never been a relic which has given rise to so much controversy, or created so much dis-

---

* This preface is not given in Sir Swâmi's translation. See *The Academy*, Sept. 1874. Nor have the two sections bringing the history of the *dalada* down to the middle of the eighteenth century been given.

† The epic poem of the *Dhâtuvaṅśa*, in the form in which it is translated by Dhammakitti Thera, is said to be considered by Siṅhalese scholars as the best specimen of the mediæval Pâli literature, and the original in Elu as "a very elaborate work, which ranks among the classics of the Siṅhalese." Some people, however, look upon it as but a poor imitation of Kâlidâsa's *Raghuvaṅśa*, possessing the same artificial style of composition in high-flown and ornate language, but not the rich imagination of the Sanskṛit poet. See *Athenæum*, Feb. 20, 1875, p. 258.

cord, between two such great religious bodies as the Brâhmaṇs and the Buddhists, as the tooth of Buddha, exerting its influence on Indian society from that reformer's death to the present time. Its adventures, trials and triumphs afford the best indications of the tenets of its persecutors, and the firm belief and superstitious tenacity of its votaries.

The history of the left upper canine-tooth, or, as vulgarly called, the left eye-tooth, may be divided into two periods, viz. the first from the death of Buddha to its removal to Ceylon, and the other from that time to the present.*

The tooth is said to have been saved from the flames by one of his disciples named Khema, while the funeral obsequies of Buddha were being celebrated at Kuinagara in the magnificent funeral pile in the forest of *sâl* trees, near the spot where he expired in B.C. 543, and whilst the princes of the surrounding countries were quarrelling for the possession of the relics.† When in his possession he was commissioned to take it to Dantapura or the Tooth-city, the capital of Kaliṅga, and deliver it over to the king Brahmadatta, who, along with his son and grandson Kari and Sunanda, greatly honoured this relic of the divine sage by offerings and festivals. In Dantapura it remained thus honoured for about eight hundred years, in spite of the Brahmanical protests against "a piece of human bone" being set up as an object of worship. At the expiration of this long period

---

* In the *Dhâtuvaṁsa* the first four cantos are taken up with the history of the relic before its arrival in Ceylon, and the fifth and last with its history in Ceylon until the close of the reign of Meghavarna. See also Forbes's *Dangistra Dalada*, *Ceylon Almanac*, 1835, and Ritter's *Erdkunde*, vol. ix., p. 201.

† Mr. Rhys Davids states that it would be interesting to know whether there is any mention of this in the *Mahâparinibbâna-Sutta*, the text of which, with a translation, is being published by Mr. Childers, while an ancient Elu work named *Thûpavaṅsa*, a history of the principal *dâgobâs* in India and Ceylon, and reckoned by the Buddhists among their sacred scriptures, although not belonging to the 'Three Baskets,' describing minutely the death of Buddha, passes over this fact quite in silence. (*The Academy*, *loc. cit.*) The former refers to the times following the attainment of *Parinirvâṇa*, or state of extinction, by Gautama Buddha, and throws some light, fragmentary though it be as a record, on the ancient history of India, and on the struggles between Brahmanism and Buddhism for supremacy in Kaliṅga in the South and Pâṭnâ in the North; the latter—a history partly of miracles, and partly of the superstitious ideas of a worship which; though loathsome, as Sir Swâmi justly observes, to the Hindu mind, and repugnant to the genius of Gautama himself—remains the sole symbol and substance of faith amongst the people, to whom the higher teachings of Buddhism are unknown, and this worship is kept up with a considerable degree of state and splendour out of the revenues derived from extensive lands and states with which their temples had been endowed in olden times by the Siñhalese sovereigns and others. It is rather interesting

we are told that Guhasiñha, a king of Dantapura, apparently ignorant of the very existence of the tooth, notwithstanding his capital being named after it, seeing one day a great festival going on in the city, inquired the cause of it, and was informed by a Buddhist priest that the people were worshipping the relic of Buddha which Khema, some eight centuries before, had brought over there. Thereupon Guhasiñha, recalled from apathy and infidelity by the remonstrances of his minister—who represented to him the unanimous belief of the people in the power of the relic—renounced heresy, and, with all the zeal and intolerance of a neophyte, persecuted and expelled from his kingdom all the Hindu devotees, called in the *Dhâtuvaṅśa* '*Niganthas*,' a sect of Śaivites elsewhere called *Achailakas* (*Ajîvakas* or naked ascetics), who had hitherto enjoyed his favour. This took place early in the fourth century of our era.

To revenge themselves for this outrage, the Niganthas repaired to the kingdom of Pâṭaliputra, modern Pâṭṇâ, and prevailed upon its sovereign —whose name is given as Pâṇḍu, and who is probably the Gautamaputra of the Satkarṇi dynasty, also called the Emperor of all India—to commission a subordinate râja named Chaitâyana to start at the head of a large army for the Kaliṅga country and bring his tributary king Guhasiñha from Kaliṅga, and the tooth, to him. This ultimatum was conceived more or less in these terms :— Whereas he (Pâṇḍu) worshipped the true gods Brahma, Vishṇu, and Maheśa, his subject Guhasiñha in Dantapura worshipped day and night a piece of bone of a dead body; therefore Guhasiñha must repair to his court, bringing the relic with him. Chaitâyana accordingly proceeded with a great army to Dantapura, where he was most amicably received by Guhasiñha, who entertained him as an honoured guest, and related the history of the relic in justification of his conversion to Buddhism. The narrative made such an impression on Chaitâyana and his officers that they requested an inspection of the wonderful relic, which being willingly complied with, Guhasiñha opened the casket, exposed the relic, and implored a recurrence of the miracles it had already wrought, which were once more repeated, and ended in the conversion both of Chaitâyana and his army to Buddhism.

---

to learn that the Siñhalese, besides the 'History of the Tooth,' are also in possession of the *Kesâdhatuvaṅśa*, the 'History of Buddha's Hair,' mentioned in the 39th chapter of the *Mahâvaṅśa*, a translation of which has been lately published in the *Journal of the Royal Asiatic Society*. They have got also the *Lalâṭavaṅśa*, or the 'History of the Frontal Bone relic of Buddha,' whose date and author are yet unknown. See *Jour. R. As. Soc.*, vol. vii., 1874.

As the order of the Emperor of all Jambudvîpa could not be disobeyed, Guhasiñha, accompanied by Chaitâyana, departed to the court of the suzerain at Pâṭaliputra, bearing with him in a splendid procession the precious relic, amidst the tears and lamentations of his people, and crossing rivers and mountains they in one time reached Pâṭaliputra. Then commenced what Buddhists term the trials of the *dalada*. Pâṇḍu, exasperated with rage at what he regarded the perversion of his army, commanded the tooth to be cast into a large pit prepared in the courtyard of his palace and filled with glowing charcoal, that it might be annihilated: "Throw now into a burning heap of charcoal," said the emperor, "the bone worshipped by this man, who has abandoned the gods worthy of adoration, and burn it without delay:" *Dhâtuvañía*, ch. iii., v. 10. The order was obeyed, but by the mystical power of the relic a lotus-flower of the size of a chariot-wheel arose above the flames, and the sacred tooth, emitting rays which ascended through the skies and illumined the universe, alighted on the top. This is supposed by a writer to explain the esoteric meaning of the Buddhist formula *Om mane padme horem*, 'The jewel is in the lotus.'* Pâṇḍu then subjected it to several other trials and indignities to destroy or dishonour it, such as throwing it into a deep and filthy ditch, which speedily became a clear pond covered with five kinds of lotus-flowers, on one of which the relic was seen reposing; burying it in the earth to be trodden down by elephants' feet, but, "spurning a subterraneous retreat and bonds of clay," it reappeared in the centre of another golden lotus-flower: thus coming out of all of these trials quite unscathed. He at last directed that the tooth should be placed on an anvil and smashed with a ponderous sledge-hammer, but the tooth penetrated and became imbedded in the anvil, where it remained safe and immoveable. The irate king, finding all efforts to extract it unavailing, then proclaimed that whoever would remove the tooth should receive a great reward. Whereupon, several persons having made attempts to extract it but in vain, a pious Buddhist, by name Subhadrâ, at last, after expounding the doctrines, and history of Buddha, evoked the relic, which immediately disengaged itself from the iron and floated in the water placed in a golden bowl which Subhadrâ held. The emperor, however, at the instigation of his

* "At that moment the tooth-relic of Buddha, ascending to the skies, and illumining all directions like the planet Venus, pleased the people, their doubts being removed."—*Dhâtuvañsa*, ver. 54. Also see *Asiatic Journal and Monthly Record*, Lond. 1838, p. 90.

advisers the Brâhmaṇs, who were persistent in saying that the bone must then be of one of the *avatârs* of their own deities,* to prevent a further succession of miracles hardened his heart and remained for some time a sceptic, uutil at the entreaty of his officers he renounced his incredulity, which also helped to confirm the wavering and convert the unbelieving, and took refuge in the *three treasures* Buddha, Dhamma, and Sangha, and built a magnificent temple for the tooth-relic, which at the close of his reign was reconveyed to Dantapura.† While all this was going on, a northern king—we are not told whence he came‡—attacked the capital in order to possess himself of the wonder-working relic, but sustained a complete defeat beneath the walls of the city and was killed. Guhasiñha returned home in triumph, but new dangers awaited him here, and fresh enemies attacked the city. He was shortly after besieged in his capital by the nephews of Kherâdhara, who had allied themselves with other chieftains. Thus having pitched their camp near the city, they sent this message, disagreeable to the ear :—"Either give us the tooth-relic of Sugata, or instantly play the war-play which confers renown and prosperity :" p. 62, *Dhâtuvañśa.* Apprehensive of the power by which he was being assailed, and seeing that resistance would be hopeless, Guhasiñha before going to the combat gave the tooth, which was the object of the besieger, in charge to Dantakumâra, his son-in-law, a prince of Avantî (Oujein), and a zealous Buddhist, and to his daughter Hemamâlâ, called also Bânavali (Hemamâlâ means literally 'a chain of gold'), enjoining them to escâpe by sea and convey it to the king Mahâsena of Ceylon, who had been for some time negotiating for its purchase; then leading his troops out against his opponents he fell in the battle. His daughter, with her husband, in the meanwhile, disguised as Brâhmaṇs, secretly conveyed the relic from Kaliṅga, buried it in the sand, as the image of Jagannâtha is said to have been in the Brahmanical accounts, then concealed it in her hair, and contriving to reach the shore took a ship from the

* "O King, there were in the world various incarnations of Janârdhana, such as Râma and the like; this bone is a part of him. If not, whence such influence as this?"—*Dhâtuvañśa*, ch. iii., v. 19.

† The king Pâṇḍu, penitent for the indignities offered to the tooth, consoled himself with the confession that he had subjected it to trials with the laudable purpose to procure triumph to true religion. "Gems," said he, "are of acknowledged perfection after they have passed through the fire; and gold becomes more valuable after its purity has been subjected to proof."—*Dhâtuvañśa*, *loc. cit.*

‡ Forbes says, king of Saewat-nuwera.—*Eleven Years in Ceylon*, vol. i., p. 216.

coast at Tâmralîpi or Tamluk, a port supposed to be situated on one of the mouths of the Ganges. The fugitives arrived at Ceylon in safety, after undergoing great hardships, and overcoming an immense number of obstacles.* This took place in the ninth year of the reign of Kṛiti Śrîmeghavarna, who reigned from 302 to 330 A.D., or, more precisely, about the year 310 A.D. The monarch, taking charge of it himself and rendering it in the most reverential manner the highest honours, deposited it in a casket of great purity made of *sphatika* stone, lodged it in the edifice called Dhâmmâchaka, built by Davananpiateva in Anurâdhapura, the ancient capital of the island, and spent an immense sum to celebrate a Dhâtâdhâtu festival, and ordained that a similar festival should be annually celebrated. The relic was then successfully transferred in procession to several shrines in Ceylon, till at last it was deposited, about the year 1268, in the Maligâva temple of Kandy, then called Śrîvardhanapura, amongst the mountains of Mâyâ, and the seat of the last native dynasty of Ceylon. It was visited by the Chinese pilgrim Fa-Hian *circa* 413 A.D., who recounts the gorgeous ceremonies with which it was carried in procession to the mountains without, &c. (Fa-Hian's *Foe Houe Si*, ch. xxxviii., pp. 334 *et seq.*)

* It would be exceedingly tiresome to enumerate these obstacles; one or two circumstances, however, are worth mentioning in detail. Halfway between the place of embarkation and Ceylon they are shipwrecked at a place called the Diamond Sands, which Mr. Fergusson supposes to be the banks of the river Krishṇa. The relic is stolen from the princess, while she is asleep, by the Nâga Râja, whose brother swallows other relics, (there were two *dronas* of relics of Buddha, besides, concealed in the kingdom of Nâga Râja), and flies to the Meru. By the power and intervention of a Thero or saint from the Himâlaya, the relic is restored and carried to Ceylon. The other relics are put into a golden cup; this is placed in a vase, and the whole put into a golden ship. A wooden ship is next built, having the breadth of a "beam of seven long cubits," and on board this vessel Hemamâlâ and Dantakumâra embark for their country. A *chaitya* is built for the relics on the Diamond Sands, which is believed to correspond with the Âmravati Topes, supposed to have been built between 322 and 380 A.D., one of the sculptures of which represents in bas-relief a ship with two persons on board, and scenes of conference between a Nâga king and a prince accompanied by a lady; and the whole presents so many points of coincidence that the story about these adventures does not appear to be apocryphal or accidental. From other sources it is apparent that a canine tooth of Buddha was deposited for some time in the Kanheri Caves in Salsette, where a copper plate supposed to be dated 324 A.D. and recording the event was discovered, and from the narrative it is extremely probable that the Kanheri tooth is identical with the one which performed so many miracles in Pâṭaliputra. Also among the Bharahut antiquities and the paintings of Ajaṇṭâ we meet with scenes of gorgeous processions carrying relics, with figures of elephants and stags, which appear to have some affinity with the processional ceremonies connected with the tooth of Buddha. For details see *Jour. R. As. Soc.*, Lond. 1868, vol. iii., p. 132; *Jour. Bomb. Br. R. As. Soc.*, vol. v., pp. 10-12; the *Indian*

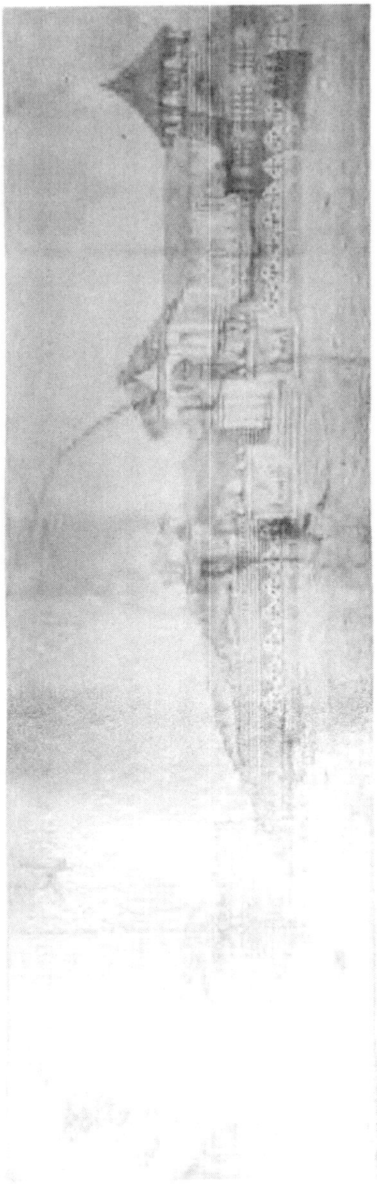

The king Dhâtusena, who reigned 459 to 477 A.D., made a jewelled casket for it.

Parâkrama Bâhu the Great, between the years 1190 and 1195 A.D., built for it a beautiful little temple at Palastipura, still extant, the exquisite workmanship of which, according to Mr. Rhys Davids, has astonished all who have seen it.

About the year 1240 A.D. Vijayabâhu enshrined it at Dambadeneyâ, whence Bhuvanekabâhu I. took it to Yâpahu, which in the opinion of Rogers is the same Yâpahu the ruins of which capital may still be seen in the Seven Korles, and is also the Yâpana of Ribeiro.

Between the years 1303 and 1314 A.D., in the reign of Bhuvanekabâhu, or about ten centuries since its reaching Ceylon under the command of a man whose name is given as Aviyachchakkarvati, Kulisekera, the king of Paṇḍi, sent an army to invade Ceylon, and got possession of the tooth and carried it from Yâpahu in the Seven Korles, which was then the capital of the island, to their country in South India, supposed to be Madura, where, however, it did not remain long, for Parâkrama III., to retrieve the loss sustained by his predecessor, went in person to Paṇḍi to treat for it, and was successful in procuring its restitution and conveying it back safely to Ceylon. His son established it in 1319 A.D. at Ḥastiselapura. It is said that it continued to be for some time close to the sacred *Bo*-tree (*Ficus religiosa*) at Anurâdhapura, the most venerated object in Ceylon, which tree is said to have been a bough of the parent tree at Uruwela, sent by King Aśoka to Ceylon, under which Buddha himself, secluded from the world in his sublime musings and meditations, had sat for six uninterrupted years—planted by King Tissa in 288 B.C., and is consequently 2163 years old*—until

---

Antiquary, vol. iii. p. 25; Mr. Fergusson's *Serpent and Tree Worship*, Lond. 1873; Cunningham's *Ancient Geography of India*, Lond. 1871, pp. 530 *et seq.* Stirling's *History of Orissa* also throws some light on the subject, especially the war that took place among Rakta, Bihar, and Sirbhum, &c. about 318 A.D.—a very near approximation to the capture and fall of Dántapura.

* Ages varying from one to five thousand years have been assigned to the Baobabs of Senegal, the Eucalyptus of Tasmania, the Dragon-tree of Orotava, and the Chesnut of Mount Etna; but all these estimates are purely inferential, whereas the age of the *Bo*-tree is a matter of record, its conservation being an object of solicitude to successive dynasties. Compared with it the Oak of Ellerslie is but a sapling; and the Conqueror's Oak in Windsor Forest barely numbers half its years; the Yew-trees of Fountains Abbey are believed to be twelve hundred years old; the Olives in the Garden of Gethsemane were full-grown when the Saracens were expelled from Jerusalem; and the Cypress of Soma, in Lombardy, is said to have been a tree in the time of Julius Cæsar; yet the *Bo*-tree at Anurâdhapura is older than the

in the year 1560 A.D. the Buddhist world was startled by hearing that it had been captured and destroyed by the Portuguese. A relic the fame of whose prodigies had filled the air, regarded by Buddhists as a sacred treasure of inestimable value, a national palladium of the Ceylonese, to fall into the hands of infidels, was truly as frightful a catastrophe as might well be imagined; no wonder then that the native authorities strongly affirm that during the fray with the Portuguese in 1560 the relic was safely hidden in different parts of the island, at Delgamoa in Saffragam, at Kandy, and at Kotmalya, &c. The Portuguese historians, on the contrary, assert that a tooth mounted in gold which had been carried to Jaffna during the commotions in the Buddhist states, believed by all the Buddhists of Jaffnapatam and elsewhere to belong to Buddha, was really brought out of the spoils of a Buddhist temple to D. Constatino da Bragança, the Viceroy of Goa, who submitted it to the Inquisition there, which tribunal ordered that it should be crushed to pieces, cast into a brazier, and the ashes thrown into a running stream, in spite of the unlimited offers in exchange for the relic, made by the wealthy monarch who ruled in further India, and who was in the habit of despatching annual embassies to pay homage to the shrine.* But I cannot do better than reproduce

---

oldest of these by at least a century, and would almost seem to verify the prophecy pronounced at the time it was planted by Tissa, that it would "flourish and be green for ever."—Sir Emerson Tennant's *Ceylon*, vol. iii., pp. 613-15, quoted almost *verbatim*; De Candolle's *Bibl. Univers. de Génève*, tome xxi. p. 394. To this tree the Ceylonese attach the deepest interest. Mr. Childers says that the *Bo*-tree occupies in modern Buddhism the same position as the cross in Christianity. The *Mahâvaṅśa* gives in too great detail the manner in which the miraculous self-severance of the parent tree took place. Chapman tells us that in 1829 the tree consisted of five principal branches, none of which appeared to exceed the 'body of a man' in thickness; and there were, besides, "smaller branches grown out of the terraces at different points" (*Remarks on the City of Anurâdhapura, Jour. R. As. Soc.* vol. xiii., p. 164.) Fa-Hian speaks of it as "letting down roots from its branches," which is more like the *Ficus Indica*; but this appears to be a mistake. We are told, again, that Buddha himself made frequent allusions to the growth of the *Bo*-tree as an emblem of the rapid propagation of his faith, just as the architectural form of the *stûpa* carried abroad another of the symbols by which Buddha used to illustrate his doctrines. About the superstitious reverence with which the tree is regarded in Ceylon the reader may see Butts's *Rambler in Ceylon*, Lond. 1841, pp. 221-242. On the right to appoint the chief priest of the sacred *Bo*-tree, and the claim that arose from the last incumbent dying suddenly from cholera without leaving any male issue, which gave rise to a trial and a historical romance similar to the Tichborne case; see the *Ind. Ant.* vol. i., p. 196.

* The fact of the capture of the tooth by the Portuguese is confirmed by the authority of Ribeiro, and by that of Rodrigues de Sá e Menezes, who in 1678 wrote his *Rebellion de Ceylan* to commemorate the exploits and death of his father, Constatino de Sá e Noronha, who perished at Badulla in 1630

here what Diogo do Couto so circumstantially tells us on the subject:—"The Viceroy, D. Constatino da Bragança, having conquered the kingdom of Jaffnapatam, went back to Goa with the king of that country fettered in irons, that were covered over with crimson velvet, and carried along with him also the sacred tooth." He then relates that "amongst the spoils of the principal temple they brought to the Viceroy a tooth mounted in gold, which was generally said to be the tooth of an ape,* but which these idolaters regarded as the most sacred of all objects of adoration. The Viceroy was immediately made aware that its value was inestimable, as the natives would be sure to offer vast sums to redeem it. They believed it to be the tooth of their great saint Buddha. This Buddha, so runs their legend, after visiting Ceylon, travelled over Pegu and the adjacent countries converting the heathen and working miracles; and death approaching, he wrenched this tooth from its socket, and sent it to

A.D. in the expedition to reduce the Kandians.—*Rebellion*, ch. i., p. 18; ch. vii., p. 99. Valentyn records also the fate of the tooth, and says it was kept near Adam's Peak till 1554.—*Beschryring van Oud en Neuw Oost Indien*, ch. xvi., p. 382. Sir Thomas Herbert, whose *Travels* were published in 1643, is truly indignant with the worship paid to the relic, and writes:—"Amongst others (which I mention only for the imposture) was that infamous Hanmant or Ape's-tooth god, which was highly esteemed and resorted to by millions of Indians till Constatino, a late Goan Viceroy, landing five hundred men at Colombo, first forcibly took away that Apish Idol, and upon their proffering a ransome of three hundred thousand duckets burned it to ashes. Notwithstanding which a crafty Bannyan so well forged another counterfeit as was believed by the Jogues to be the same (willing to be deluded, it seems), thereby exceedingly enriching himself, and joying not a little these simple Zeylonians."—*Some Years' Travels*, Lond. 1665, p. 359. Francis Pyrard de Laval, who visited Ceylon about 1608, relates the event as having occurred during the revolt of D. Joaõ (Modeliar?), which is posterior to the capture of the tooth-relic. The story of this revolt appears to have been treated in detail by Diogo do Couto in his XI. Decada, which unfortunately has been lost. For important documents on the subject the *Archivo Portuguez-Oriental*, Fasc. 30, may be consulted with advantage.

* Faria y Souza also states it to be the tooth of an ape, and a white ape (*Monó blanco*) besides, and according to Sir Emerson Tennant the facsimile at Kandy resembles the tooth of a crocodile rather than that of a man. The word 'ape' is further said to arise from confounding Buddha and Hanuman, the monkey-god.—Sir E. Tennant's *Ceylon*, vol. ii., p. 201. In the *Asia* of Faria y Souza I read the following:—"El venia a ser un diente de Mono blanco. Parece que este color, por improprio, ò inusitato en algunos animales, se haze no solamente admirabile, mas aun divino quando se halla en ellos. El aver solido blanco de las manos de la Naturaleza un Elefante del Rey de Siam, fue causa de codiciarlo el Bramà de Pegù; y la codicia dél, lo vino a ser de gran derramamiento de sangre entre aquellas dòs Naciones. Acà estotra blancura en el Mono vino a ser la ceguera (ciega mucho lo blanco en que son frequentes los ojos) de inumerables Almas. Finalmente siempre el Mundo se pierde por bestias amadas con excesso de los Principes dèl."—Cap. xvi., p. 350.

Ceylon as the greatest of relics. So highly was it venerated by the Siñhalese and by all the people of Pegu that they esteemed it above all other treasures.*

"Martin Alfonso de Mello happening to be in Pegu with his ship on business when the Viceroy, D. Constantine, returned (to Goa) from Jaffnapatam, the King, hearing that the tooth which was so profoundly revered by all Buddhists had been carried off, summoned Martin Alfonso to his presence and requested him, as he was returning to India, to entreat the Viceroy to surrender it, offering to give in exchange whatever might be demanded for it. Those who knew the Peguans, and the devotion with which they regarded this relic of the devil, affirmed that the King would willingly give three or even four hundred thousand cruzados† to obtain possession of it. By the advice of Martin Alfonso, the King despatched ambassadors to go in his company to the Viceroy on this affair, and empowered them to signify his readiness to ratify any agreement to which they might assent on his behalf.

"Martin Alfonso, on reaching Goa in last April (1561), apprised the Viceroy of the arrival of the envoys. The Viceroy,‡ after receiving

* Decada VII., liv. ix., cap. ii., pp. 316 *et seq.* of the edition of 1783.

† *Cruzado*, so called from its bearing a cross, being coined at the period of the Crusades, is worth two shillings and nine pence.

‡ The Viceroy, D. Constantino de Bragança, was the fourth son of D. Jaime, fourth Duke of Bragança and a prince of the reigning dynasty of Portugal. He left Lisbon for India, when only 31 years old, on the 7th April 1558, and arrived at Goa on the 3rd September of the same year, and on landing took the usual oath as Viceroy of India. His name has remained dear to the Indo-Portuguese, as he was firm, wise, and benevolent. He has incurred, no doubt, the censure of the historian on account of the famous tribunal of the Inquisition being established in Goa during his government, but he had no hand in that affair, which was settled long before in Portugal. His piety is shown in his building the church of St. Thomas, in the Campo de S. Lazaro, in the old city of Goa, where it was his intention to enshrine the relics of the apostle St. Thomas, discovered by one Manoel de Faria, described in ancient documents as the Captain of the Coromandel Coast, in 1523, in the town of Meliapur; but the inhabitants of that place objected to their removal. The church, however, could not be finished during his stay in India, and is now in ruins, although in 1827 it allured the Abbé Cottineau to say mass at its altar on the day of the Apostle, 15th December. (See his *Journal* in the *Instituto Vasco da Gama*, 1874, p. 260.) He admitted into intimate friendship the unfortunate poet Camoens, and through his politeness and good sense silenced those who were trying to procure the banishment of the satirist, whose *Disparates na India* had severely handled certain persons of influence in Goa. The Viceroy took an active part in those expeditions which were periodically sent to Ceylon and elsewhere for the propagation of Christianity, especially that of Jaffnapatam, which had been some years before fervently preached as a sacred vow by St. Francis Xavier, and for which he had to travel from Cochin to Bassein (see my *Notes on the History and Antiquities of Bassein*, *Jour. Bomb. Br. R. As. Soc.* 1874, p. 328). D. Constantino governed

them hospitably, opened the business for which they were sent by their king. They began the conversation by making a request for the tooth on behalf of their sovereign; offering in return any terms that might be required, with a proposal for a perpetual alliance with Portugal, and an undertaking to provision the fortress of Malacca at all times when called upon to do so, together with many other conditions and promises. The Viceroy promised an early reply, and in the meantime communicated with his veteran captains and fidalgos, all of whom were of opinion that so great an offer should be accepted, which would replenish the exhausted treasury; and so eager were they, that the question seemed to be decided.

"But the matter having reached the ear of the Archbishop, Don Gaspar,* he repaired instantly to the Viceroy, and warned him that he was not to permit the tooth to be ransomed for all the treasures of the universe, since it would be dishonouring to the Lord, and would afford an opportunity to these idolaters to pay to that bone the homage that belonged to God alone. The Archbishop reminded him often of the subject, and even preached against it from the pulpit in the presence of the Viceroy and all his court, so that Don Constantino, who as a good Catholic feared God and was obedient to the prelates, hesitated to proceed with the affair, or to take any step that was not unanimously approved of.

India until the 7th September 1561, and in January 1562 embarked on board his ship, the Constantina, which had doubled the Cape of Good Hope seventeen times, brought four Viceroys to India, and lasted altogether 25 years—a rare feat of navigation in those days: *Oriente Conquistado*, Dec. XI., cap. i., p. 193. His government was altogether prosperous, and the King, D. Sebastiaõ, whose offer to D. Constantino of the Viceroyalty of India for his lifetime had been politely declined, said to the Viceroy D. Luis de Ataïde on his second nomination to that post, "Allez," as Lafitau expresses it, "gouvernez comme a fait Don Constantine!" A very good portrait of the Viceroy D. Constantino is in the Governor's palace at Pangim or New-Goa, one at Damaun, one in Faria y Souza's, and another in Lafitau's works.

* D. Gaspar de Leaõ Pereira was a canon of the see of Evora who came to Goa as Archbishop in 1560 A.D. It was he who held the first consecration of bishops in the church of St. Paul, assisted by the Patriarch of Ethiopia and the Bishop of Malacca. The priest consecrated was a Jesuit by name Melchior Carneiro, Bishop of Nicæa, and a coadjutor of the abovenamed Patriarch. In the evening of the day of consecration he baptized in the church of *Santa Fé* 409 persons of the province of Salsete of Goa, in the presence of the four prelates. At that time Salsete contained only one church and a mission-house at Rachol, but at the end of fifty years it could boast of twenty-eight. The Patriarch could never reach Abyssinia, which circumstance induced him to resign his title and assume that of Bishop of China and Japan. He died in Macao about two years after his nomination.—*Bosq.*, *Hist. de Goa*, pp. 77 *et seq.*

"He therefore convened an assembly of the Archbishop, the prelates, divines, and heads of the religious orders, together with the captains, senior fidalgos, and other officers of the government, and laid the matter before them, saying that by the large offers of money that had been made for the tooth the pressing want of the state would be provided for.* After mature deliberation among all those theologians, who had it well studied beforehand, a resolution was come to, that it was not proper to part with the tooth, since its surrender would be an incitement to idolatry, and an insult to the Almighty—sins that should not be committed though the state, or even the world itself, might be imperilled. Of this opinion were the divines—the Archbishop; the Inquisitors, Fr. Antonio Pegado, Vicar-General of the Dominicans, Fr. Manuel da Serra of the same order, the Prior of Goa, Rev. Custodio de San Francisco, and another theologian of the same order; Rev. Antonio de Quadros, of the Company of Jesus, the Provincial of India; Rev. Francisco Rodrigues o Manguinho of the same order, and several others.

"Having resolved thus, and committed it to writing, to which all attached their signatures, and a copy of which is now in our possession in the Record Office (or in the Torre do Pombo),† the Viceroy called on the treasurer to produce the tooth. He handed it to the Archbishop, who, in their presence placed it in a mortar, and with his own hand reducing it to powder, cast the powder into a brazier which stood ready for the purpose, after which the ashes and the charcoal together were scattered into the river, in sight of all who were crowding the verandahs and windows which looked upon the water.

"Many protested against this measure of the Viceroy, since there was nothing to prevent the Buddhists (*gentios*)‡ from making other idols; and out of any piece of bone they would shape another tooth in resemblance of the one they had lost, and extend to it the same worship;

* Some of these fidalgos wished to carry the relic themselves back to Pegu, and collect money on the way by exhibiting it to the Buddhist worshippers. Faria y Souza recounts this story, and Lafitau repeats it. "Ninguno dudava ya de que ella se haria, y muchos descubrieron la codicia de ser cada qual embiado a Pegù con el diente vendido, para ir mostrandole a los Gentiles por todas las Poblaciones que ay de una a otra parte, y juntar un Tesoro de las ofertas con que era creible avian de acudir todos a adorarle."—Faria y Souza *Asia Portugueza*, cap. xvi. on "Hazaña heroica y augusta del Vi-Rey D. Constantino," p. 352; Lafitau, *Hist. des Découv. et Conq.*, tome iv., p. 232.

† It does not exist at all.—*Boletim do Governo de Goa*, 1858, p. 660.

‡ The Portuguese apply the term *Gentio* (a Gentile) indiscriminately to a native of India, unless he is converted to Christianity or Mahomedanism.

whilst the gold that had been rejected would have satisfied the pressing needs of the state. In Portugal itself much astonishment was expressed that these proceedings should have been assented to.

"To commemorate the event, and to illustrate the spirit which had dictated an act approved by the Fathers of the Company, and signalized by zeal for Christianity and the glory of God, a device was designed as follows:—On an escutcheon was a representation of the Viceroy and the Archbishops surrounded by the prelates, monks, and divines who had been present on the occasion, and in the midst was the burning brazier, together with Buddhists offering purses of money, and above, the letter C, being the initial of Don Constantino, was repeated five times, thus—

C C C C C

and below it the five words—

Constantinus, cœli, cupidine, cremavit, crumenas—

the interpretation being that 'Constantine, devoted to heaven,' rejected the treasures of earth.' "*

One can easily imagine the effect this imposing assembly of the Viceroy, prelates, and the notables of the old city of Goa, met for the purpose of pounding a piece of bone to dust, would have on the minds of the populace thronging the streets, the dismay of the wretched Peguan embassy at the sight of the destruction of their saint's relic, and the grim exultation of the stern Inquisitors over the dissolution of the *dalada* in the sacred waters of the Gomati, and the consequent promotion of the glory of God, the honour and prestige of Christianity, and the salvation of souls. If there ever was a point where two extremes met, it is this. The burning of a tooth for the glory of the Almighty was the point of contact between the sublime and the ridiculous. However, the doers of such an act took pride in it, and had a scutcheon made to commemorate their heroic deed. *Suum cuique.*

In later times the transaction appears to have been estimated in various ways, the clerical element delighting in the reminiscence of it, and the lay characterizing it as a fanatic and foolish action.

But it is difficult to please all. The Rev. Denis Louis Cottineau de Kloguen, a French missionary, writes:—"Constantine is also blamed and ridiculed for having refused to give to the king of Pegu

* Decada VII., liv. ix., cap. xvii., page 428 *et seq.*

a tooth (which some affirm to have been that of a monkey), but which had been revered as that of Buddha in a temple of Jaffnapattana in Ceylon, although that prince offered for it 300,000 cruzados; in this business Constantine acted as a conscientious and religious man; he consulted the Archbishop and clergy on this occasion, as he was afraid on the one hand of participating in an act of idolatry and superstition, and on the other of defrauding the King his master of a considerable treasure; and when it was made clear to him that, according to conscience and natural reason, it was unlawful to participate in an act of idolatry for any reason whatsoever, much less for a sum of money, which would be adding to the former guilt that of avarice, he immediately consented that the infamous relic should be thrown into the sea. If he had taken the money, he would certainly have been represented by prejudiced authors as a covetous man without law or conscience; but as he acted otherwise they call him a fool. It is very difficult, or rather impossible, to please those who are bent on blaming their fellow-creatures."*

But those were not really far from truth who thought that the Buddhists would shape another tooth out of any piece of bone. Long before the Peguan embassy's return home the Siñhalese had found out the tooth. Some said, as writes Padre Francisco de Souza in his *Oriente Conquistado,* that the moment the Archbishop placed the tooth in the mortar and was about to pulverize it, it made its way through the bottom and went straight to alight on a lotus-flower in Kandy, where they have built for it a temple called Dalidagis, or temple of the sacred tooth. Others revived a facsimile not only in a duplicate, but in a triplicate form of the desecrated relic.

The story of the resuscitated tooth is of some importance, and is also minutely related by Couto, who writes:—"At the birth of Brahma, king of Pegu, the astrologers who cast his nativity predicted that he

* *Historical Sketch of Goa,* pp. 33, 34.

† "Fingem os chingalas que o dente de Budu sahira pelo fundo do almofariz, quando D. Constantino (naõ; o arcebispo) o quiz desfazer, e se fora pôr em Candia sobre uma formosa rosa, e assim lhe dedicaram um famoso templo chamado Dalidagis, que significa 'casa do dente sagrado."—*Oriente Conquistado;* Conquista I., Divisaõ I., No. 82. The same author narrates the whole affair as minutely as Couto. His work, however, is very rare, and scarcely known, I believe, to English scholars. The work of Texeiro Pinto on the causes of the decadence of the Portuguese possessions in Asia has also a recriminatory article on the subject, as he thinks the Portuguese Viceroy should have accepted the ransom-money proffered by the Buddhist king, which would have replenished their (in those times) empty coffers. But the priests reply to this with their warped and threadbare argument that "he was a freemason."

would marry a daughter of the king of Ceylon, who was to have such and such marks and features, and certain proportions of limbs and figure. Brahma, willing to fulfil the prediction, sent ambassadors to Don Juan (the king of Cotta), whom he addressed as the sole inheritor of the royal blood and the only legitimate sovereign of the island, and requested his daughter in marriage, accompanying the demand by a shipload of rich presents, consisting of things unknown in Ceylon, besides woven cloths and gems. The envoys arrived about the time that the king had abandoned Cotta to take up his residence within the Fort of Colombo (A.D. 1564). He received the ambassadors with much distinction, and, apprised of their mission, concealed from them the fact that the astrologers were in error, as he was childless. He had, however, brought up in his palace a daughter of his great chamberlain, a prince of the royal blood who had embraced Christianity through the instrumentality of the governor, Francisco Barreto, who had stood his godfather and given him his name; and such was the influence of this man, in addition to the claim of relationship, that in all things the king was directed by his advice. This girl the king treated with every honour as his own child; on the arrival of the envoys she had a place assigned to her at the royal table, and was addressed as his daughter, and under that designation he sought to make her wife to the king of Pegu. The opposition which he apprehended was from the Captain-General of Colombo and the Franciscans, who, although the girl was a Buddhist, might nevertheless regard her as a lamb within their fold, whom they could any day induce to become a Christian, and they were, therefore, likely to interfere to prevent her leaving the island. Discussing these considerations with the great chamberlain, who was a man of resources and tact, the latter pointed out to the king, who relied on his judgment in all things, that although forced to abandon Cotta, and reduced to poverty, he might, through this alliance, open up a rich commerce with Pegu; and he accordingly assented that the girl should be despatched to the king, provided she was conveyed away secretly and without the knowledge of the Portuguese at Colombo.

"But the chamberlain did more; in concert with the king he caused to be made out of a stag's horn a facsimile of the ape's tooth carried off by Don Constantine, and mounting it in gold he enclosed it in a costly casket, richly decorated with precious stones. Conversing one day with the Peguan ambassador and the Buddhist priests (talapoens) in his suite, who were about to set out to worship and make offerings at the sacred footprint on Adam's Peak,* the chamberlain, who was a Buddhist at heart, disclosed to them in confidence that Don Juan, the Siñhalese king, was still in possession of the genuine tooth of Buddha,† that which was seized by Don Constantine being spurious, and that he, the great chamberlain, kept it concealed in his house, the king of Ceylon having become a Christian. The ambassador and the talapoens evinced their delight at this intelligence, and besought him to permit them to see it; he consented reluctantly, and, first obliging them to disguise themselves, he conducted them by night to his residence, and there exhibited the tooth in its shrine, resting on an altar, surrounded by perfumes and lights. At the sight they prostrated themselves on the ground, and spent the greater part of the night in ceremonies and superstitious devotion; afterwards, addressing the great chamberlain, they entreated him to send the relic to the king of Pegu at the same time with the princess, undertaking that, as a part of the splendour and pomp of the marriage, Brahma would send him a million of gold, and year by year despatch to Ceylon a present of a ship laden with rice and such other articles as might be required. All this was negotiated privately, the king and the great chamberlain alone being in the secret.

"When the time arrived for the young lady to take her departure, it was so cunningly arranged that neither the Captain of Colombo, Diogo de Mello, nor the priesthood suspected anything. Andrea Bayam Moodliar accompanied her as ambassador from the sovereign of Ceylon, and after a prosperous voyage they landed at a port to the south of Cosmi, and announced their success and the arrival of the queen, to the

---

* Adam's Peak, in Ceylon, is the place where Buddha, on his arrival in the island, was invited by Santana, the guardian of the mountain, to leave an impression of his foot, the celebrated Śrī Pada ('beautiful footstep'), which has attracted travellers to the summit of the mountain from very remote times. Marco Polo alludes to it, and says it is so steep and precipitous that men are only able to mount to the top with the help of massive iron chains fixed to it. The footprint is a hole in the rock about five feet long, and represents a very rude outline of a foot. Still this does not prevent Buddhists from claiming it as the foot of Buddha, Śaivites as that of Śiva, Mahomedans as that of Adam, and Christians as that of St. Thomas. See Mr. Skeen's account of it; Hardy's *Manual*, p. 212; Alabaster's *Wheel of the Law*, p. 252; and Marco Polo's *Travels*, vol. ii., pp. 256-7. Mr. Skeen, a resident in Ceylon and the author of *Adam's Peak*, had in preparation, I am told, an elaborate work on the subject I am writing about—the Tooth-Relic of Ceylon; but most unfortunately, before the work was finished, he died suddenly about three years ago.

† Couto calls the tooth "*Dente do seu idolo Quijay*," in another place "*do Quiar*," which according to Tennent is the corrupt spelling of the Burmese *Phra*, another name for Buddha, or a modification of the Chinese Keu-tau.

delight of the king and his nobles. * * * The son and heir of the king received her as she disembarked * * * the king met her at the gates of the palace which was assigned to her as a residence, gorgeously furnished in chamber, antechamber, and wardroom with all that became the consort of so rich and powerful a monarch, who conferred upon her immense revenues to defray the charges of her household. For days he devoted himself to her society, conducted her to the royal residence, and with great solemnity required the people to swear allegiance to her as their queen. The eunuchs who waited on her imparted these particulars to Antonio Toscano, with whom they were intimate, and who communicated them to me.

"But as in these countries no secret is long preserved which is in any one's keeping, King Brahma came at length to discover that his wife was the daughter, not of the king, but of his chamberlain; for it seems that Andrea Bayam, the Siñhalese ambassador, who, as the proverb says, could not keep his tongue within his teeth, divulged it to some Chinese at Pegu, who acquainted the king. He, however, was little moved by the discovery, especially as the talapoens and ambassadors gave him an account of the ape's tooth, and of the veneration with which it was preserved, and of the arrangement which they had concerted with the person in charge of it. This excited the desire of Brahma, who regarded it as the tooth of his idol, and reverenced it above everything in life; even as we esteem the tooth of St. Apollonia (though I shall not say much of the tooth of that sainted lady); more highly than the nail which fastened our Saviour to the cross, the thorns which encircled his most sacred head, or the spear which pierced his blessed side, which remained so long in the hands of the Turks, without such an effort on the part of the monarchs of Christendom to rescue them as King Brahma made to gain possession of this tooth of Satan, or rather of a stag. He immediately despatched the same ambassadors and talapoens in quest of it, and sent extraordinary presents by them to the king of Ceylon, with promises of others still more costly. The ambassadors reached Colombo, negotiated secretly with Don Juan, who placed the tooth with its shrine in their hands with much solemnity and secrecy, and with it they took their departure in the same vessel in which they had arrived."* Again he continues:—

"In a few days they drew near to Cosmi, a port of Pegu, whence

* Decada VIII., cap. xii., pp. 74 *et seq.*

the news spread quickly; the priesthood (talapoens) assembled, and the people crowded devoutly to offer adoration to the tooth. For its landing they collected vast numbers of rafts elaborately and richly ornamented, and when they came to carry the accursed tooth on shore it rested on gold and silver and other costly rarities. Intelligence was instantly sent to Brahma at Pegu, who despatched all his nobles to assist at its reception, and he superintended in person the preparation of a place in which the relic was to be deposited. In the arrangements for this he displayed to the utmost all the resources and wealth at his command. In this state the tooth made the ascent of the river, which was covered with rich boats, encircling the structure, under which rested the shrine, so illuminated that it vied with the brightness of the sun.

"The king, when all was prepared, seated himself in a boat decorated with gilding and brocaded silks; he set out two days in advance to meet the procession, and on coming in sight of it he retired into the cabin of his galley, bathed, sprinkled himself with perfumes, assumed his most costly dress, and on touching the raft which bore the tooth he prostrated himself before it with all the gestures of profound adoration, and on his knees approaching the altar on which rested the shrine, he received the tooth from those who had charge of it, and raising it aloft placed it on his head many times with adjurations of solemnity and awe; then restoring it to its place, he accompanied it on its way to the city. As it passed along, the river was perfumed with the odours which ascended from the barges, and as it reached the shore the talapoens and nobles of the king, and all the chief men, advancing into the water, took the shrine upon their shoulders and bore it to the palace, accompanied by an inpenetrable multitude of spectators. The grandees taking off their costly robes spread them on the way, in order that those who carried that abominable relic might walk upon them.

"The Portuguese who happened to be present were astonished on witnessing this barbarous pomp; and Antonio Toscano, who I have stated elsewhere was of the party, has related to me such extraordinary particulars of the majesty and grandeur with which the tooth was received, that I confess I cannot command suitable language to describe them. In fact, everything that all the emperors and kings of the universe combined could contribute to such a solemnity, each eager to display his power to the utmost, all this was realized by the acts of this barbarian king.

"The tooth was at last deposited in the centre of the courtyard of the palace, under a costly tabernacle, upon which the monarch and all his grandees presented their offerings, declaring their lineage, all which was recorded by scribes nominated for that duty. Here it remained two months till the vihâra which they set about erecting could be constructed, and on which such expenditure was lavished as to cause an insurrection in the kingdom.

"To end the story, I shall here tell of what occurred in the following year, between the king of Kandy and Brahma, king of Pegu, respecting these proceedings of Don Juan, king of Ceylon. These matters which Don Juan had transacted so secretly, touching the marriage of his pretended daughter with the king of Pegu, as well as the affair of the tooth, soon reached the ear of the king of Kandy, who, learning the immense amount of treasure which Brahma had given for it, was influenced with envy (for he was a connection of Don Juan, having married his sister or, as some said, his daughter), and immediately despatched an envoy to Pegu, whom the king received with distinction. He opened the object of his mission, and disclosed, on the part of his master, that the lady whom Don Juan had passed off as his own child was in reality the daughter of the great chamberlain, and that the tooth, which had been received with so much pomp and adoration, had been fabricated out of the horn of a deer; but he added that the king of Kandy, anxious to ally himself with the sovereign of Pegu, had commissioned him to offer in marriage a princess who was in reality his own offspring, and not supposititious; besides which he gave him to understand that the Kandyan monarch was the possessor and depository of the genuine tooth of Buddha, neither the one which Don Constantine had seized at Jaffnapatam, nor yet that which was held by the king of Pegu, being the true one,—a fact which he was prepared to substantiate by documents and ancient *olas*.

"Brahma listened to his statement, and pondered it in his mind; but seeing that the princess had already received the oaths of fidelity as queen, and that the tooth had been welcomed with so much solemnity and deposited in a vihâra specially built for it, he resolved to hush up the affair, to avoid confessing himself a dupe (for kings must no more admit themselves to be in error in their dealings with us than we in our dealings with them). Accordingly he gave as his reply that he was sensible of the honour designed for him by the proffered alliance with the royal family at Kandy, and likewise by the offer of the tooth;

that he returned his thanks to the king, and as a mark of consideration would send back by his ambassadors a ship laden with presents. He caused two vessels to be prepared for sea, with cargoes of rice and rich cloths, one for Don Juan, and the other for the king of Kandy; and in that for Don Juan he embarked all the Portuguese subjects whom he had held in captivity, and amongst them Antonio Toscano, who has told me these things many times. These ships having arrived at Ceylon, the one which was for the Kandyan port had her cables cut and was stranded before she could discharge her cargo, so that all was lost and the ambassador drowned; some said that this was done by order of the Siñhalese king, Don Juan, and if so it was probably a stratagem of the great chamberlain, for the king himself had no genius for plots. Thus things remained as they were, nothing further having been attempted or done."*

The next curious episode in the history of the tooth-relic and the religious annals of Ceylon is the apostasy, or reversion to his former faith, of Dom Joaõ, and his seizure of the *dalada* as crown property. The Portuguese having roused the Kandyans to revolt against their king, Râja Siñha, Kanapû Bandar of Paradencia, a political intriguer and Siñhalese of royal blood, who had been educated at Goa by the Jesuits and had embraced Christianity under the name of Dom Joaõ, was despatched with an armed force to enthrone Dona Catherina, the daughter of the fugitive king Jayaweira. The expedition was successful, and the Portuguese made arrangements for conferring the sovereignty on Dom Felipe, on whom they desired to bestow the hand of Queen Catherina, which arrangements, however, Dom Joaõ did not agree to. The consequence was that he turned his army against his allies, driving them away from Kandy, and removed his rival by poison. Thus left undisputed master of Kandy, D. Joaõ then seized on the supreme power, defeated the army of his native opponent, Râja Siñha, who had threatened to inflict on D. Joaõ the same torture as that under which his father had expired—that of being buried underground up to the neck and then the sufferings terminated by rolling huge stones on the head above the surface—and assumed the Kandyan crown under the fantastic name of 'Vimala Dharma.' Then he gave the last finish to his policy by abjuring Christianity, which secured to the usurper the support of the Buddhist priesthood, and raised the superstructure of his fortunes

* Decada VIII., cap. xiii., pp. 83 *et seq.* Although Sir Emerson Tennent has given these extracts from Couto in his work on Ceylon, I have drawn mine from the original and have compared them with his.

by producing the *dalada,* without which, as the national palladium inseparable from royalty, he could not venture to gain the suffrages of his people. It was the same *dalada* discovered by Vikrama Bâhu, and the apostate did not fail to persuade the Kandyans, already prone to believe it, that this was the original or genuine relic, which at the arrival of the Portuguese had been removed from Cotta and preserved at Delmagoa, while the one destroyed by the Portuguese was a counterfeit. This is the very relic that is now exhibited in the temple at Kandy.*

In spite, however, of all the circumstantial external and internal evidence, proving that the invaders had seized the relic, and that the priests in Goa, with the Archbishop at their head, had really opposed this traffic in idols as impious, and that their piety was triumphant in the scattering of the *dalada's* ashes into the waters of the Mandovi, there are not a few, although not Buddhists, who think that the Portuguese had really been imposed upon. Mr. Rhys Davids is one of them; he writes:—"Jaffna is an outlying and unimportant part of the Ceylon kingdom, not often under the power of the Siñhalese monarchs, and for some time before this it had been ruled by a petty chieftain; there is no mention of the tooth brought by Dantakumâra having been taken there,—an event so unlikely and of such importance that it would certainly be mentioned had it really occurred. We have every reason to believe, therefore, that the very tooth referred to in the work edited by Sir Coomara Swami is preserved to this day in Kandy."† But that the relic was at the same time within the range of the Portuguese army is also quite patent; for the Siñhalese chronicles had no need to mention that during those troublous times the relic was concealed in Delmagoa, in Saffragam, and elsewhere, if it was so secure in its sanctuary of the Maligâva temple. And then, again, while thus roving about the island, might not their genuine *dalada* have actually fallen into the hands of the Portuguese? And if spurious, then the king of Pegu had no necessity to offer such a handsome amount of money for it, which fact has not been denied. The dimensions and form of the *dalada,* the clumsy substitute manufactured by Vikrama Bâhu in 1566 to replace the original burnt by the Portuguese in 1560, are, moreover fatal to any belief in its identity with the one originally worshipped. The present *dalada* is said to resemble the tooth of a crocodile, as the old one was asserted to be that of a monkey. But it is neither. It is but

---

* Ribeiro, *Hist. d'Isle de Ceilan,* bk. i., ch. v.

† *The Academy, loc. cit.*

a curved piece of discoloured ivory, as Sir E. Tennent rightly observes, about two inches in length and more than one in diameter, which unexampled dimensions are by Buddhists accounted for by a strange argument, that in the days of Buddha human beings were giants, and their teeth kept pace, so to speak, with their larger stature.*

Dr. Davy, who, it appears, was one of the first Christians to see the modern *dalada*, in 1817 describes it thus:—"It was of a dirty yellow colour, excepting towards its truncated base, where it was brownish. Judging from its appearance at the distance of two or three feet (for none but the chief priests were privileged to touch it), it was artificial, and of ivory, discoloured by age."† Major Forbes saw it again on the 28th May 1828, during the great Kandyan festival, in company with Sir Robert and Lady Horton and party, amongst whom was Baron von Hugel. He writes:—"It is a piece of discoloured ivory, slightly curved, nearly two inches in length, and one in diameter at the base; from thence to the other extremity, which is rounded and blunt, it considerably decreases in size." ‡ Elsewhere he continues:—"Not the least curious fact connected with this antique is, that the original promoter of the imposition (which passed it as a tooth of Gautama) did not procure some old man's tooth, and thus deprive sceptics of at least one strong argument against its authenticity."§

* As regards the stains now observed in the relic, we are told that the Buddhists claim them as a proof of identity, from the fact of their having been made the subject of remark centuries ago by the king Pându, as recorded in the *Dhatuvanśa*. But its yellowish-brown colour, if it then existed, could not possibly have inspired the following allusion in the same epic:—"The tooth-relic, of a colour like a part of the moon, white as the *kunda* flower (a species of jasmine) and new sandalwood, caused with its radiance palace-gates, mountains, trees, and the like to appear for a moment as if of polished silver."—Canto v., ver. 63. Only the faith of a Buddhist can explain away these discrepancies.

† Davy's *Account of Ceylon*, Lond. 1821, p. 368.

‡ Forbes's *Eleven Years in Ceylon*, Lond. 1820, vol. i., p. 293. The same author has published in the *Ceylon Almanack*, 1835, an article on this subject entitled "The Dangistra Dalada, or Right Canine Tooth of Gautama Buddha," but this is erroneous. All other authorities concur in calling it the left canine, which is moreover qualified as belonging to the upper set by naming it the left eye-tooth. In reference to other canine teeth Col. Yule writes:—"Of the four eye-teeth of Śâkya, one, it is related, passed to the heaven of Indra, the second to the capital of Gandhâra, the third to Kaliṅga, the fourth to the snake-gods. The Gandhâra tooth was perhaps, like the alms-bowl, carried off by a Sassanide invasion, and may be identical with that tooth of Fo which the Chinese annals state to have been brought to China in A.D. 530 by a Persian embassy. A tooth of Buddha is now shown in the monastery of Fuchau, but whether this be either the Sassanian present, or that got from Ceylon by Kublai, is unknown. Other teeth of Buddha were shown in Hwen Thsang's time at Balkh and at Kanauj."—Yule's *Marco Polo*, vol. ii., p. 266.

§ Forbes's *Eleven Years in Ceylon*, vol. ii., p. 220.

Both Dr. Davy and Major Forbes have given a drawing of it; that of the latter, slightly reduced in size, appears to have been reproduced by Sir E. Tennent in his charming *History of Ceylon*, and by Col. Yule in his excellent edition of *Marco Polo's Travels*. The following diagrams, copied from the above-mentioned works, along with a faithful representation of the permanent human upper canine tooth, show at once the palpable difference there is between the tooth of a man and the counterfeit one now exhibited in Kandy.

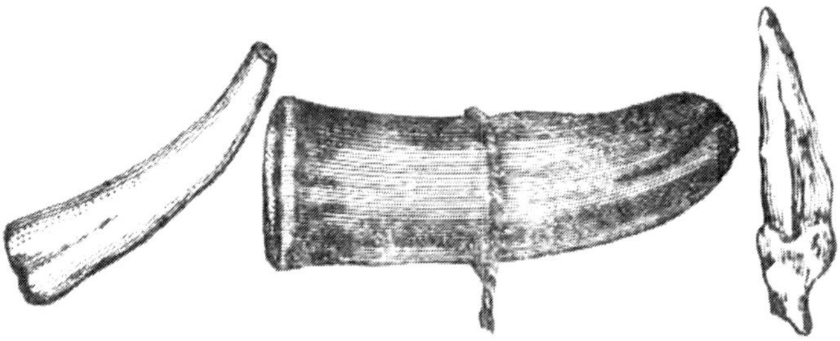

After Dr. Davy. After Major Forbes. Human canine tooth.

The human canine teeth, or cuspids as anatomists call them, are about three-quarters to one inch in length, and consist of three parts, viz. the crown, the neck, and the fang or root. The crown is thick, conical, convex in front and hollowed behind. The point or cusp is generally blunted or becomes worn down by use. The neck is contracted, and as such only slightly marking the separation between the crown and the root. The fang is single, conical in form, compressed laterally, and lined by a slight groove on each side. It is evident that both in size and form the human tooth bears a striking contrast to the one at Kandy.

Now a few words about the temple and sanctuary where the tooth-relic is deposited. If the Buddhists persist in saying that it is the tooth of Buddha, as they always will, then they have every reason to be proud of their Maligâva temple, where it rests after having had its wanderings and returns, captivities and exiles, degradation and triumphs, during two thousand years of travel. No relic, as Bishop Heber truly remarks, "was ever more sumptuously enshrined or more devoutly worshipped."*

* *Narrative of a Journey*, &c. vol. ii., p. 254. The venerable Bishop also mentions that although he did not see the tooth, he was shown a facsimile, which is more like a wild beast's tusk than a human tooth.

Dr. Davy, who was in Kandy in 1817, describes the temple where the tooth-relic is now preserved, thus:—" The dalada Malagawa was the domestic temple of the king, and is the most venerated of any in the country, as it contains the relic, the tooth of Buddha, to which the whole island was dedicated, and which is considered by good Buddhists as the most precious thing in the world. Tho temple is small, of two stories, built in the Chinese style of architecture. The sanctum is an inner room, about twelve feet square, on the upper story, without windows, and to which a ray of natural light never penetrates. You enter it by folding doors, with polished brass panels, before and behind which is a curtain. The splendour of the place is very striking; the roof and walls are lined with gold brocade; and nothing scarcely is to be seen but gold, gems, and sweet-smelling flowers. On a platform or stage about three feet and a half high, and which occupies about half the room, there is a profusion of flowers tastefully arranged before the objects of worship to which they are offered, viz. two or three small figures of Buddha,—one of crystal, and the other of silver gilt,—and four or five domes or caskets, called karanduas, containing relics, and similar in form to the common Dagobah. * * * All but one of the karanduas are small, not exceeding a foot in height, and wrapped in many folds of muslin. One is of much greater size, and uncovered, and with its decorations makes a most brilliant appearance. It is five feet four and a half inches high, and nine feet ten inches in circumference at its base. It is of silver, from three-tenths to four-tenths of an inch thick, and gilt externally. It consists of three different pieces, capable of being separated from each other. Its workmanship is neat but plain, and it is studded with very few gems, the finest of which is a valuable cat's-eye on the top, which is rarely seen. The ornaments attached to it are extremely rich, and consist of gold chains, and a great variety of gems suspended from it. The most remarkable of these is a bird hanging by a gold chain, and formed entirely of diamonds, rubies, blue sapphires, emeralds, and cat's-eyes, set in gold, which is hid by the profusion of stones. Viewed at a little distance, by candle-light, the gems about the karandua seem to be of immense value, but when closely inspected they prove in general to be of bad quality, and some of the largest merely crystal coloured by a foil. This great karandua is the receptacle of the dalada, 'the tooth,' as it is considered, of Buddha. * * * Never was relic more preciously enshrined; wrapped in pure sheet-gold, it was placed in a case, just large enough to receive it, of gold, covered externally with emeralds, diamonds, and rubies, tastefully arranged. This beautiful and very valuable bijou was put into a very small gold karandua, richly ornamented with rubies, diamonds, and emeralds: this was enclosed in a larger one also of gold, and very prettily decorated with rubies: this second, surrounded with tinsel, was placed in a third, which was wrapped in muslin; and this in a fourth, which was similarly wrapped: both these were of gold, beautifully wrought, and richly studded with jewels. Lastly, the fourth karandua, about a foot and a half high, was deposited in the great karandua."*

But to return to the history of the *dalada*. In 1815 A.D. the relic came, along with the island of Ceylon, into the possession of the British Crown. The first Adhikar (Minister of State and Justice) remarked on this event that whatever the English might think of the consequences of having taken Kappitapola (a rebel chief of Ceylon), in his opinion and in the opinion of the people in general the taking of the relic was of infinitely more moment."† And Dr. Davy remarks: "The effect of its capture was astonishing, and almost beyond the comprehension of the enlightened."‡ For the powers of the tooth as a national palladium, somewhat similar to those which in the thirteenth century obtained among the Scotch concerning the stone at Scone, and which are even nowadays current in Goa concerning the body of the greatest missionary Portugal ever sent to the East,§ and the exemption of Ceylon from foreign domination as long as it possessed the relic and the sacred tree at Anurâdhapura, are oracularly propounded in the *Râjaratnâkarî*, and as fully believed by the Siñhalese Buddhists.

* Davy's *Account of Ceylon*, pp. 366-69.

† Forbes, vol. ii., p. 221.

‡ Davy, p. 369.

§ The tradition about the body of St. Francis Xavier being the palladium of the liberties and independence of the Goanese, and in the hands of whose silver image, placed on the north-facing altar of his mausoleum, an official *bâtôn* is deposited, and reverentially taken possession of by each new Governor on taking charge over of the state, as one of the insignia inseparable from government, draws support from several puerile legends. One of these is to the effect that when in 1801 a British auxiliary force, without any hostile intention, was posted at Agoada and Cabo during the political commotions in Europe caused by the great Napoleon, and remained there until the general peace in 1815, a man in the habit of a friar was seen almost every night in the encampment striking with his knotted cord the men and officers of the force. Resistance was impossible, for their tormentor, although visible, was strangely impalpable; and the force, unable to bear any longer the tortures of this implacable friar, were obliged suddenly to beat a retreat. The ghost in the habit of a friar is said to have been St. Francis Xavier, who, fearing foreign invasion, thus compelled the British to decamp.

During the rebellion against the English in 1818, in which again the relic played an important part, it was clandestinely removed by certain priests appointed to officiate at its sanctuary, but towards the conclusion of the rebellion it was again restored, having been found with a priest who was seized in the Matale district, by the care of the British Government, who then empowered its Resident at Kandy to act as the custodian of the relic, and a soldier to keep guard every night at the door of the temple.* It was at last entirely surrendered to the British, together with the Kandyan kingdom, in 1825. The next occasion on which the *dalada* attracted attention was at its public exhibition in Kandy on the27th of May 1828, the first time after fifty-three years since the king Kṛiti Śrî had openly displayed it, on which occasion a considerable sum of money was collected from the assembled multitude of devotees, who flocked thither from all parts of the country to worship the relic. Of this splendid festival and procession we have numerous records. On that day all three larger cases having previously been removed, the relic contained in the three inner caskets was placed on the back of a richly caparisoned elephant, over it a small octagonal cupola or canopy supported by silver pillars, and all this grand apparatus carried round in solemn and gorgeous procession. For details the reader may peruse with advantage Lieut.-Col. Colebrooke's article on the subject of processions in the *Jour. R. As. Soc.*, Lond. 1836, vol. iii., pp. 161-64, which is as follows :—

"On the full-moon day of the month Vaiśākh (Thursday, the 29th of May 1828), the principal chiefs and other Kandyans, zealous professors of the Buddhist religion, celebrated the festival Dalada Pinkawa, when the following arrangements were made :—

"The *maṇḍapa* or pavilion erected for the reception of the relic and its attendant priests measured 229 feet by 60; and that part assigned for the place of the relic was adorned with valuable stuffs embroidered with gold and silver. In the centre of the pavilion was a silver seat, on which was placed a *ransiligey*, or golden frame, containing an artificial flower of gold, of dazzling lustre, and intended to hold the relic; on the right was a large golden *karandu*, or case, set with precious stones, and on the left a smaller one similarly ornamented.

"These two cases were ornamented with precious stones, such as rubies, sardonyx, &c., of great value. In front of this was the offertory

---

* *Revue des deux Mondes*, 1854, p. 143.

decorated with silk and embroidered cloths; and before it were nine veils of various cloths of gold and silver, and rows of frills made of fine cloth. The part of the pavilion appropriated to the priests was decorated with white cloths and white cocoanut leaves.

"The pavilion erected for the Europeans was sixty feet by thirty; that for the Siñhalese chiefs of the high and low countries one hundred feet by thirty; both of these were also decorated with white cloths and white cocoanut leaves.

"These pavilions were erected on a plain near the palace, and surrounded by fifty-three arches of honour, ornamented in various ways; besides which on the arches were erected flagstaffs, designated as follows:—One for each of the *Desavoni* of the four Korles, and of Matelle, and one for the *Maligáwa*, or temple. These flags were of red, white, and various colours.

"A proclamation having been made by beat of *tom-tom* for decorating the streets in Kandy, many devout people, with a view of surpassing each other in the beauty of their decorations, embellished the streets most elegantly, and anxiously awaited the first day of the festival. On the morning of this day soldiers were ordered on guard at the corners of the streets and at watch-stations.

"At half-past ten A.M., the officers, chiefs, and *Desaves*, clothed in silk, and decorated with golden chains, proceeded to the temple in which the relic was kept, in grand procession as follows:—

"First, a flag belonging to *Gajanaike Nillame, Lekams*, and *Desaves*; then *tom-tom* beaters; next musicians; then whip-crackers; * then the *Maha Nillame*, having in his hands a *Katupulle-rattan* worked in gold; the *Matelle Desave*, and *Maha Gabuda Nillame*, each with a silver dagger in his hand; then followed drum-beaters, trumpeters, and *chańk*-blowers; † next, officers in palanquins, attended on each side by public singers; and then the Siñhalese chiefs and head-men on foot. From the gate of that pavilion to that of the temple, head-men of the Desavonis and Rátas, armed with daggers, and the *Mudeliárs* and *Mohandirams* of Kandy, dressed in their respective uniforms, were

* "In Ceylon it is customary for persons of rank when going into public to be preceded by a number of men bearing whips, with which they keep up a constant cracking. The lash of the whip is very long, curiously twisted, and tapering to a point; the handle is short and thick. Specimens of these whips are to be seen in the Museum of the Royal Asiatic Society.

† "The *chańk*-shell, *śańkha*, or conch (*Voluta gravis*), used by the priests all over India instead of a trumpet. They are esteemed sacred, and there is a regular fishery for them off the north-west coast of Ceylon.

ranged in two ranks. In this order the procession came to the gate and stopped; when the chief priest of the shrine of the relic brought it forth, and all kinds of music and firing of cannon began, with shouts of the thousands of people assembled there, exclaiming *sádú! sádú!* corresponding with our 'amen.' These three different and united sounds echoed through the air like thunder. Amidst the rejoicings the case or shrine containing the relic was borne under a canopy towards the elephant trained to carry it; when the many Buddhist spectators of this splendid object were transported with joy, and, with tears trickling down their cheeks, gave a shout so tremendous that the simultaneous discharge of twenty-five pieces of ordnance was inaudible.

"Thus the shrine was conveyed with great pomp to the elephant, and handed to the *Maha Nillame*, who gave it over to the hands of the *Desaves* of *Matelle* and *Udapalata*, who were on the back of the elephant, and who, having placed it in the case intended for its reception, dismounted.

"The procession was again arranged in the following order:—

"*1st*—Two state elephants: then a flag bearing the device of an elephant, and hand-flags; and then a chieftain and his people.

"*2nd*—The great flag, accompanied by a chieftain with a silver dagger in his hand, and his people.

"*3rd*—The sun and moon flag of the great chieftain of the four Korles, hand-flags, a silver cane worked in gold, and the people of that chieftain.

"*4th*—The lion-flag and hand-flags of the seven Korles, accompanied by their chieftains and people.

"*5th*—The white flag and hand-flags of the chieftain of *Matelle*.

"*6th*—The silk flag and the hand-flags of the chieftain of *Suffragám*.

"*7th*—The flag and hand-flags of the chieftain of the three Korles.

"*8th*—The peacock-flag and hand-flags of the chieftain of *Wallapone*.

"*9th*—The lotus-flag and the hand-flags of the chieftain of *Udapalata*.

"Then came, in order, the flags of the *Maligáwa*; *tom-tom* beaters; musicians; drummers and trumpeters; *chaṅk*-blowers; men bearing torches of various descriptions: an elephant covered with a sheet embroidered in gold; a silver umbrella; a silver shield; an elephant covered with a sheet embroidered in silver; a silver umbrella; a silver shield; an elephant of state covered as the last; a silver umbrella; a silver shield; whip-crackers, followed by officers of state; torchbearers; then the elephant conveying the relic, over which was spread a flowered canopy; the officers of the temple parading on foot around the elephant, each having a worked *talapat,** or leaf, in his hand.

"On the right and left of this elephant were the several great officers of state, mounted on elephants covered with scarlet, embroidered in gold and in silver, with flags, bearing devices, worked on the richest and brightest embroidered silks, with shields of gold, and umbrellas of silver.

"Thus the procession, leaving the gate of the temple, proceeded through several streets, and returned to the pavilions on the plain, when the two chiefs who placed the shrine on the elephant took it off, and handed it back to the *Mahá Nillóme,* who conveyed it to the pavilion. No sooner was this done than different kinds of music, shouts, and the discharge of cannon recommenced. The shrine was then given over to the hands of the chief priest, who carried it to the seat before described, removed the relic from the thirteen gold cases in which it was deposited, and placed it on the golden flower.

"The relic was exhibited first to the English ladies and gentlemen, and then to the priests, who, like a poor man finding a precious stone, beheld it with ardent looks and inexpressible joy, crying aloud, *sádú! sádú!* and worshipping it. After these and many other ceremonies were performed, the relic was again deposited in the case, about the tenth hour of the night.

"On the following day, about one o'clock, all the chiefs, clothed in white, proceeded to the place where the relic was. It was then taken out of the case, and the chiefs worshipped it, and offered money, cloth, &c. Vocal and instrumental music, with dancing, then followed. After this, people of the high and low countries worshipped the relic seven days, and made offerings to it; during which time it was guarded thus:—

"First, the chief priest and seven other priests kept near the seat on which the relic was; these were enclosed with a row of veils; out-

* "The leaf of the great fan-palm (*Corypha umbraculifera*), used as a parasol or screen."

side of these veils were seven chiefs armed with silver daggers; then another row of veils and guards; then a third row of veils and guards; then a company of Malays; then guards; and, lastly, police officers.

"On the night of the third day, about ten o'clock, there were fire-works, rope-dancing, and fencing with swords and shields, &c. &c.

"On Thursday, the 3rd of June (till which day the relic was exhibited and offerings made), at ten o'clock, the case containing the relic was carried back, with the same procession as before, from the pavilion to the temple, and the celebration ceased.

"All the ceremonies that were performed by the chief priest when the relic was taken out were repeated when it was brought back from the pavilion to the temple."*

In 1834 a secret plan was concerted by some disaffected Siñhalese to remove again the *dalada,* and renew the scenes the Kandyan country had once witnessed so grievously in 1818; but these proceedings were carefully watched by the Government, the delinquents arrested, and thus the scheme was frustrated. For a long time afterwards the relic was in the official custody of the Ceylonese Government, and Turnour was the first European, it appears, who, for more than nine years, had the keys of the sanctuary constantly in his library, save during the performance of the daily offerings. It is only within a few years, *circa* 1839, that, owing to the remonstrances of the Christian societies in England, the connection of the existing Government with the shrine has ceased.

In 1858 two Burmese bonzes from Rangoon were sent to Ceylon by the king of Burma on a mission almost similar to that of his remote predecessor the king Anavantha, who in the eleventh century had sent an embassy to endeavour to procure the relic, but could obtain only "the miraculous emanation" of it, to contain which a tower in the palace-court of Amarapura was built. This time the priests went there to get a facsimile of the tooth, which they obtained, on the 9th October of that year, and the whole transaction is but a repetition *mutatis mutandis* under the British of what, about three hundred years ago, took place under the Portuguese. The latter, swayed by the Inquisitional influence and perhaps scruples of conscience, not only refused to give up but burnt the relic; the former, more tolerant, if not more enlightened, allowed the model to be taken, which has since been deposited

* *Jour. R. As. Soc.*, Lond. 1836, vol. iii., pp. 161-64.

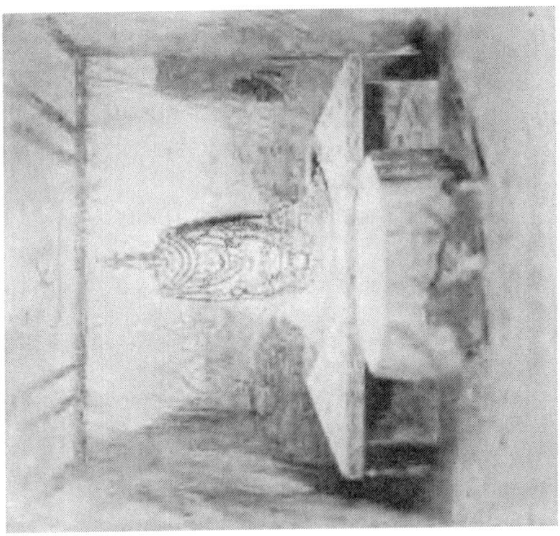

within the walls of the palace at Mandalay, the new capital of Burma.*

The present condition of the sanctuary and its precious contents require a few words of description. We are told that "nothing can be more picturesque than the situation and aspect of Kandy, on the banks of the miniature lake overhung on all sides by hills which command charming views of the city with its temples and monuments below." But the sanctuary of the great relic, notwithstanding the beauty of the scenery around, and its richness in gems and precious metals, is a small chamber without a ray of light, in which the air is stifling hot and heavy with the perfume of flowers, situated in the inmost recess of the *vihâra* attached to the palace of the Kandyan kings. The frames of the doors are inlaid with carved ivory, and on a massive silver table hung round with rich brocades stands the bell-shaped *karandua*, the shrine or dâgobâ, consisting of six cases, the largest or external cover, five feet in height, formed of gilt silver inlaid with rubies and other gems, and ornamented with jewelled chains; other caskets, similarly wrought, but diminishing in size gradually; until on removing the innermost one, about one foot in height, a golden lotus is disclosed, in which reposes the mystic tooth. In front of the silver altar a plain table is placed for people to deposit their gifts upon. These *karanduas* are said to have been made for the relic by successive sovereigns between 1267 and 1464 A.D.

The last event in the history of the *dalada* is the solemn visit paid but a few months ago by the Burmese envoys to the Maligâva temple at Kandy on their return from Europe, in fulfilment of the special commands of their king. The pomp and circumstance of that splendid pilgrimage evoked a fresh enthusiasm in the Siñhalese for their revered tooth-relic, and numerous were the tokens of obeisance and devotion offered to the shrine.

What stirring times has not the *dalada* gone through during the twenty-five centuries which have elapsed since it was first picked up from the Kuśinagara funeral pile of the great sage, while monarchs were fighting for its possession, until its present comfortable lodging in the richest shrine raised by man to a mistaken devotion; and what a part has it not played in the religious history of India, from the

† *Madras Examiner*, 26th August 1858. Conf. also Col. Yule's *Marco Polo's Travels*, vol. ii., p. 265, and *Revue des deux Mondes*, 1860, p. 129, where a graphic description of the ceremony is given, and the relic is described thus:—"C'est un fragment d'ivoire de la dimension du petit doigt, jaune fauve, un peu courbé vers le milieu, et plus gros à une extrémité qu'à l'autre."

epoch in which Buddhism became the dominant faith of the country, subsequently persecuted and tyrannized over by a powerful enemy, ruined by the degeneracy of its own adherents, and enfeebled by schism and heresy, until at last all disasters culminated in its being banished from its birthplace to find a refuge in distant foreign lands! Then, its place usurped by the stern dominion of El Islâm, spreading its faith throughout the fair plains of Hindustân by the merciless edge of the sword, to be followed by a still sterner race, "that nation of heroes," as the Abbé Raynal called the Portuguese, coming from the far West to supplant "the nation of philosophers," as Professor Max Müller designates the Hindus; and who by the discordant use of the torch, the symbol of barbarism, on the one hand, which marked its passage by the lurid flames of burning cities, and of the cross, the emblem of peace, on the other, which by the persuasive voice of the missionary they succeeded in planting all along the coast of our peninsula, named, as if to add insult to injury, the very sacred tree of Buddha *Arbor diaboli* or Devil's-tree.* In bringing this incomplete Memoir to a close, I cannot more fittingly conclude than in the words of the learned Rodier, who says:—"Les règlements orgueilleusement immuables, pour le corps et pour l'âme, que les théocrates de l'Inde ont eu la témérité d'imposer à la société, ont fini par y détruire tous les éléments du progrès. Le génie indou, autrefois si brillant, si fécond, si vivace, meurt étouffé dans une camisole de force.

"Le dur contact de notre civilisation le réveillera peut-être. Espérons que les déscendants des Arias trouveront, tôt ou tard, une compensation aux douleurs et aux humiliations que leur inflige la préponderance des Européens; qu'ils nous emprunteront la foi en la puissance et en la légitimité des efforts individuels, et qu'ils apprendront de nous à se mouvoir en dehors des limites conventionelles de leur vieille organisation. Puissent les pères des nations modernes reprendre un jour une place honorable dans l'édifice dont ils ont, avec tant de patience, établi les fondements!"†.

---

* Rheede's *Hortus Malabaricus*, vol. ii., pp. 46-7, fig. 27.

† G. Rodier's *Antiquité des Races Humaines*, pp. 372-373.

INDEX.

K.

L.

M.

Corrigenda.

Page 6,	line 40,	*for* Jagganâtha	*read* Jagannâtha.
16	30	sensation	sensations.
31	33	Amaravati	Amarâvatî.
34	12	Kuinagara	Kuśinagara.
36	13	Dhâtuvania	Dhâtuvaṅśa.
40	14	Constatino	Constantino.
40	23	Tennant's	Tennent's.
41	34	Fasc. 30	Fasc. 3.
41	44	solido	salido.
46	38	Texeiro	Texeira.

Works by the same Author.

INTRODUCÇÃO ao ESTUDO da SCIENCIA da VIDA. Bombay, 8vo, 1868.

DENGUE, its HISTORY, SYMPTOMS, and TREATMENT; with observations on the Epidemic which prevailed in Bombay during the years 1871-72. Bombay, 8vo, 1872.

(See the *Lancet*, vol. i., p. 365, 1873.)

NOTES on the HISTORY and ANTIQUITIES of the ISLAND of BASSEIN. Bombay, 8vo, 1874.

Only a few copies obtainable.

Messrs. THACKER, VINING & Co., Bombay.